*A Model
for a
Better Future*

A Model for a Better Future

KIM ALEXIS
with Jim Denney

A
JANET
THOMA
BOOK

THOMAS NELSON PUBLISHERS
Nashville

Published in Nashville, Tennessee, by Thomas Nelson, Inc., Publishers.

Scripture quotations noted NKJV are from THE NEW KING JAMES VERSION. Copyright © 1979, 1980, 1982, 1990, Thomas Nelson, Inc., Publishers.

Scripture quotations noted NIV are from the HOLY BIBLE: NEW INTERNATIONAL VERSION®. Copyright © 1973, 1978, 1984 by International Bible Society. Used by permission of Zondervan Publishing House. All rights reserved.

Library of Congress Cataloging-in-Publication Data
Alexis, Kim.
    A model for a better future / Kim Alexis with Jim Denney.
        p.   cm.
    ISBN 0-7852-6857-X
    1. Alexis, Kim. 2. Christian biography—United States.
3. Models (Persons)—United States—Biography. 4. Christian
life. I. Denney, James D. II. Title.
BR1725.A645A3   1998
248.4'092—dc21
[B]
                                                      98-31532
                                                      CIP

Printed in the United States of America.

1 2 3 4 5 6 BVG 04 03 02 01 00 99 98

*I would like to dedicate this book
to my mother, Barbara,
who gave up eighteen years of her life
to be my model for a better future.*

*And to my husband, Ron,
who taught me how to stand up and speak
the truth.*

And especially to Jesus who is the Truth.

Contents

Acknowledgments

This book came together with a gentle nudging from God. God knew that I had something special to share with you.

I want to thank Janet Thoma for feeling that nudge, too, and believing that I had something worthy to say that others needed to hear.

Jim Denney, God placed you in my path to voice my thoughts and beliefs. You knew what I wanted to say, and without you this book would not have been written.

Ray Manzella, my manager, thank you for understanding that I need to turn down "certain jobs."

Mom and Dad, you did a great job as parents. Thank you.

Ron, you are my other half. Without you I don't feel complete.

And a special thanks to my children—James, Bobby, Noah, Amber, and Shay—who have made me a mother. What a neat job it is to raise you all.

1
My Unplanned Life

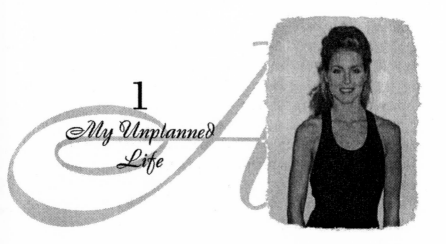

"Life," someone once said, "is what happens to you while you're making other plans." That is absolutely true. I know.

Let me tell you how life happened to me.

I was seventeen, in my senior year in high school in Lockport, near Buffalo, New York. Unlike a lot of my peers, I knew exactly where I was going in life. I had picked out my college, my major, and my career.

I was going to be a pharmacist.

I had already selected the University of Rhode Island, and I was accepted into the five-year pharmacy program. I had visited the campus and stayed overnight with the girls on the swim team. Having been a competitive swimmer for twelve years, from age six through my senior year at Lockport Senior High, I wanted to continue swimming in college.

So I was all set. I had my life all planned out. I knew where I was going and what I would be doing.

I wanted to have a measure of independence when I went to college—I wanted some "fun money" of my own, and I didn't want my dad to have to pay for everything. As I was trying to decide what I could do to make money on the side, people kept telling me, "You're pretty—you ought to try modeling."

"Is there money in that?" I asked.

"Oh, yes!" I was told. "Lots of money!"

So I called several modeling agencies, and they told me I needed to go to charm school or modeling school first. The best one I could find in the area was in Buffalo, about a thirty-minute drive from my home. So I started my first course at charm school—it cost about $500 for a ten-week course, two hours one night a week.

The first thing they had me do was take a "before" picture. I remember being very self-conscious and uncomfortable in my little leotard. I didn't know how to stand, how to pose, what to do with my hands—I just felt completely awkward. During the course, they taught me things I never imagined I would have to learn—how to walk, how to sit in a chair, how to open and close a door, how to enter a room. I would go home and practice all these actions—and I thought it was all so silly.

I felt awkward and inferior at charm school—like a fish out of water. I saw the other girls in the school as much more polished and experienced than I was. A number of them had been on the runway in fashion shows, and had thick portfolios of photos. Modeling was not just a sideline to them—it was their life's dream.

I wasn't happy at charm school. I just felt I had to endure it in order to get into a modeling agency. I finished my first course and started a second course—another ten weeks, another $500.

"I've Got My Life Planned"

One night, I came to class and was surprised to see a very short, odd-looking man sitting in the front of the class. Throughout the class, he sat and stared at me, which made me feel very self-conscious. No one bothered to explain who he was or why he was there.

That evening, the lesson was on how to walk down the runway. Throughout the class, I tried to forget the little man in the front row and simply to focus on what we were learning. At one point, however, the owner of the charm school—a very tall, regal, elegant woman—called me out of the class and led me to her office.

My mind was whirling. My first thought was that I had really messed up, and that they were going to kick me out of the charm school! Now I'd never get to be a model! At the same time, I tried to remember all the lessons they had taught me—how to walk, how to stand, how to open and close the door, how to sit—in the hope that they might let me stay.

The owner indicated a chair in the office and I sat down, being careful to place my hands in my lap as I had been instructed. As I sat down, the odd little man also came in and sat down. *What is this all about?* I wondered.

The man looked at me appraisingly, addressed me by name, and introduced himself. Then he asked, "How would you like to go to New York and work as a model?"

"You mean, modeling full-time," I asked, "as a career?"

"That's right," he said.

"No, thank you," I said. "I'm only taking this class so I can be a model part-time while I'm going to college. I never wanted to do it for a career. I've got my life planned. I'm going to be a pharmacist."

He blinked in astonishment. "You're kidding me!" he said. I don't suppose he got turned down very often. "Do you realize that I am a talent scout for a major New York modeling agency? This is a very important career opportunity I'm offering you!"

"Well, I don't want to seem ungrateful," I said, "but my mind is made up—I'm going to be a pharmacist."

I really didn't want the life of a professional model. I had a mental picture of what a model's life would be like—going to bed every night with cold cream all over my face, my hair in rollers, filing my nails all the time. Yuck! That was not for me! A little modeling on the side was one thing—a few local fashion shows, maybe some local advertising work, I could endure that—but a professional model? Me? No way! I would hate that!

I saw myself as a swimmer, an athlete, not a glamour girl. I didn't wear makeup very much and I always had wet hair, and I was just not into all those beauty things.

The little man from New York City left that night—but he came back two more times, and each time he tried to coax me to change my mind. Finally, on his third try, I reluctantly agreed to consider his offer. My parents were away on a vacation cruise at the time, and my grandmother was staying at the house with me. I told the man, "When my parents get home, I'll discuss it with them, and we'll call you."

"Excellent!" the man said. "Now, we need to take some photos that I can show to the people at the agency in New York."

I sighed. "Oh, all right," I said. "Take your pictures." I picked out some outfits for the photo session, and the man snapped dozens of shots, then went away happy.

Several weeks passed. Meanwhile, my parents returned home and I told them about the man from the New York agency. None of us thought it was a big deal or that anything would come of it.

Then one day the phone rang. It was a woman from the Elite modeling agency in New York. "Miss Alexis?" she said. "Would you hold, please? Mr. Casablancas would like to speak to you." John Casablancas was the owner of the agency—one of the largest and most prestigious modeling agencies in the world.

We talked, and he told me of the great plans he had for my future. I told him I had different plans. I was going to be a pharmacist.

"Kim, Don't Ever Say, 'I Could Have . . .'"

On March 29, 1978—a date that is forever etched in my memory—Mr. Casablancas came to Buffalo amid a swirl of publicity and hype. There were newspapers covering his arrival in town. He told the press that he had come to Buffalo to discover a model. That night, I went to my scheduled charm school lesson as usual, unaware that Mr. Casablancas would be there, along with several newspaper reporters and photographers.

Mr. Casablancas carried on as if he were planning to sift randomly through the modeling prospects in Buffalo and pick the best girl he saw. What I didn't know was that he had really come to Buffalo specifically to recruit me. He was hoping that when he picked me in such a public way, in front of the media, there would be so much pressure on me to accept that I would not be able to say no.

So there I was at charm school, feeling completely intimidated and inferior—and there was Mr. Casablancas, standing in front of the class, the head of one of the top agencies in the world. He talked to the class for a bit, then he asked me to come up and stand next to him. He had all the other girls' portfolios in front of him, and he began going through them in front of the class. I didn't even have a portfolio. In fact, the only photos that had ever been taken of me were the ones the Elite agency's talent scout had taken some weeks before.

As he went through the portfolios, he kept turning to me, showing me this or that girl's photos, and saying, "What do you think about this one? Or this one? Do you like this one?" He was asking me to critique the other girls in the class—and I was intimidated by them! I felt inferior to them!

I kept saying, "Oh, that's a great picture. And that one's nice."

But he'd frown and shake his head. "No," he kept saying, "that's not what I'm looking for."

And he had the girls parade past, showing how they walked and conducted themselves. But he kept saying, "No, that's not what I'm looking for."

The whole time, I was thinking, *What am I doing up here? Why does Mr. Casablancas keep asking for my opinion? I don't know anything. I'm just a green kid from Lockport—these girls have all the talent and experience. They want to be models. I want to go to college and be a pharmacist.*

Throughout the session, the press had been there, taking pictures. When it was over, John Casablancas took me and my parents into the office and the four of us sat down and talked. He talked to us for a long time, telling us what I could expect from a career as a professional model. He wanted to ease any concerns my parents had—after all, I was just seventeen and still in my senior year in high school. He made me an offer that agencies never make anymore: a one-year contract with a guarantee of $500 a month, whether I worked or not.

"That's how confident I am that you're going to make it big," he said. "Kim, you're going to be a big star."

Five hundred dollars a month! I had been making $1.98 an hour as a clerk in a drugstore in Lockport—cleaning shelves, working the cash register, and blushing with embarrassment whenever anyone would come to the register with a package of Tampax or a jockstrap. A lot of girls wouldn't have taken two seconds to make the decision that confronted me: working in a drugstore or becoming a model in New York—decisions, decisions!

But I couldn't decide! I had my life planned! I was going to be a pharmacist! After all that planning, it wasn't easy for me simply to jump in a totally new direction.

Then my dad looked at me and said something I've never forgotten: "Kim, don't ever say, 'I could have . . .' Don't ever say, 'If only . . .' I don't want you to ever look back on your life and say, 'I could have done this, I should have done that.' Just go for it. You can put college off for a year. We'll write the university a letter, and ask them to hold a place for you. But this is too big an opportunity to pass up."

"Okay," I said at last, turning to John Casablancas. "I'll go to New York. But I want to finish my senior year of high school, and I want to stay for my eighteenth birthday—I'll come to New York right after that."

"Well," he said, "don't wait too long. We need you."

As we walked out to the parking lot, my mind was whirling. I couldn't believe the turn my life was taking. I hadn't sought a modeling career—if anything, it had sought me! I was perfectly fine with my life, my friends, my plans, everything—but suddenly, I was headed for New York and an entirely new set of possibilities.

But then, as we were saying good-bye to John Casablancas, he turned to me and said something that absolutely shattered me: "By the way, Kim, you need to lose fifteen pounds."

Fifteen pounds!

Never in my life had I given any thought to my weight or my figure. If I had felt insecure before, I suddenly felt devastated! How was I going to lose fifteen pounds?

It wasn't as if I could drop those pounds by exercising. I was already getting as much exercise as I could cram into my schedule! How many girls my age were lifting weights—especially in the 1970s? But I was lifting weights, on top of swimming five and a half hours a day. I was a dedicated swimmer, and our Lockport High swim team was the best in the state. My four years there, from the ninth grade through the twelfth, *we were undefeated in every single meet.* I was part of the team that placed first in the state for the 400-yard medley relay, plus I got ninth place in the state for the 100-yard butterfly event. I was a dedicated athlete. I swam both before school and after school, and I was already in shape for competition— I just didn't have fifteen pounds to spare!

I've always been a big, muscular girl—not the typical thin waif image most people associate with the modeling industry. To top it off, in those days, there weren't all the diet programs and diet books we have today. The only way I could drop fifteen pounds was by starving myself. To this day, I can't keep those fifteen pounds off—and to this day, I can hear John Casablancas say, "By the way, Kim, you need to lose fifteen pounds." That's been the thorn in my flesh, the hole in my self-esteem, ever since that day.

For years afterward, I tried every weird, fad, panic diet that came along, trying to keep those fifteen pounds off.

My Real Name

My eighteenth birthday was July 15, 1978. On July 17 I flew from Buffalo to New York, along with my parents. They were in the seats behind me, and I sat next to a friendly, talkative, older man. He reminded me of a leprechaun—he was Irish and he was short and he gave me his business card, which was printed in shamrock-green ink. He asked me why I was going to New York, and I told him that I was going to sign a contract with a modeling agency. "Well, well!" he said. "You're embarking on something very big, young lady—and you're going to be a star!" I couldn't imagine how he could be so sure, but it sounded nice—even though I wasn't sure I wanted to be a star.

We arrived in New York and my parents helped me get settled in my own hotel—they stayed in a different hotel down the street. They wanted me to get established in my own place. A lot of girls who were with the Elite agency roomed together at that hotel.

After I got settled, we went to the agency. I remember walking with my parents into John Casablancas's office—a plush corner office with an incredible view of the city. John greeted us warmly. After I filled out some forms and signed the contract, John said to me, "Now what do you want to be called?"

I looked at him blankly. "Well," I said, hesitating, "Kim. I want to be called Kim Alexis. That's my name."

He shrugged. "Okay—but you know you can use any name you like."

"I'll just stick with Kim," I said—but I winced inwardly. *Ooh,* I thought, *I probably just stuck myself with a boring name. Maybe I should have come up with something more exotic!*

But after I became successful, people always asked me, "What's your real name?" And I'd have to say, "My real name is Kim Marie Alexis—that's the name I was given when I was born." Everyone marvels. They tell me it's the perfect celebrity name. Maybe so, but it wasn't planned that way.

I'm glad I didn't change it. John Casablancas made it sound as if I had entered a fantasy world—I could become whomever and whatever I wanted to be. I could even change my name!

Luckily, I was so naive and so small-town practical, it never occurred to me to be anyone but who I was: Kim Alexis from Lockport.

Kelly and Me

I immediately became friends with another model, Kelly Emberg, who was one of my roommates. She was a year older than I, and had come to New York only a month before I did. Though Kelly would later achieve supermodel status, date rock superstar Rod Stewart, and appear in hundreds of magazines, we started out together as a couple of wide-eyed kids in the big city. Kelly is very sweet and very funny, and even though she was older, I felt she needed looking after. To this day, she's one of my dearest friends—and I'm still looking after her!

Early on, the agency would assign us to "test shoots," photo sessions for which neither the model nor the photographer gets paid. The photographer gets the use of a beautiful model, and the model gets to use the photos to build her portfolio, so they help each other out. I didn't have to do many test shoots—I was getting paid work very early, so I didn't really need them.

But Kelly and I did accept a test shoot assignment with a pair of French photographers who were brothers. Because there would be no one from the agency with us at the shoot, Kelly and I were both a little gun-shy about the assignment. We decided to go together—safety in numbers. But early on, the two brothers started acting a little funky—making sexual suggestions and smutty comments. That was enough—we called a halt to it and walked out.

A few days later, Kelly and I were on the street in New York, looking for something to eat—something cool and light, because it was a hot August in New York, and we were both trying to stay thin. As we were looking for a deli, we spotted something down the block—a film crew shooting a movie. Neither of us had ever seen a movie being made before, so we elbowed our way through the crowd and asked a man with the film crew who was in the movie. We were hoping it was some big star, and when the man said the star was Desi Arnaz Jr., that was big enough for us. He said, "Come on over, I'll introduce you to Desi."

So we went over, met Desi, and talked to him for a while. Within five minutes or so, he invited us to go with him to Studio 54, the big New York nightclub with the exclusive clientele. "I'll pick you up around midnight," he told us. So he did, and we ended up with him at Studio 54.

We stayed up all night, dancing and having a great time. There was a lot of boozing and cocaine snorting going on. People offered us drinks and coke, but Kelly and I just had ice water. We were old enough to drink, but we didn't want it. We just kept dancing and having a great time, operating on sheer youth and energy alone.

At five in the morning, Kelly and I raced home and she called her parents and I called mine. I had awakened my mom and dad, of course, but they were happy to hear from me. I told them everything—that we had met Desi Arnaz Jr., and he had taken us dancing at Studio 54, and there were drugs there but we didn't take any, blah-blah-blah. After saying they were thrilled for Kelly and me and glad we said no to drugs, my parents hung up and went back to bed.

My parents didn't worry about me being in that environment. They knew I was sensible and could handle myself, and as long as I was openly telling them about everything I saw, they didn't have anything to worry about. In time, however, I stopped telling them everything. There were some things I did that I wasn't proud of.

While this book was being written, Desi Jr. and I cohosted a charity tennis event in Industry Hills, California. It was the first time I had seen him in years. My husband, Ron, and I were talking with him, and I said, "Desi, do you remember when you were shooting a movie in New York City—it was twenty years ago almost to the day—and you met a couple of young models and took them out to Studio 54? That was Kelly Emberg and me."

Well, Desi didn't remember. Of course, in those days, he probably took a lot of young models out to Studio 54! "Just tell me one thing," he said. "Did we kiss?"

"No!" I replied. "We did *not* kiss!"

He looked at Ron and shrugged. "Well, darn, I tried!"

Actually, he didn't try. This may not be good for Desi's image as a ladies' man, but he was actually very nice and gentlemanly toward Kelly and me that entire evening.

My Plans Versus His Plans

I look back on those early days of my modeling career, and the one feeling that comes flooding back, as fresh as if it were yesterday, is a feeling of utter insecurity and vulnerability. I felt like a fish out of water when I was at charm school, I felt the same way when I got into the modeling world, and to some extent, I even feel that way today.

People don't realize that, even after all the magazine covers, ads, fashion shows, television shows, and movies, I still don't see myself as "Supermodel Kim Alexis." Inside, I know I'm still just Kim from Lockport—a walking mass of insecurities and vulnerability.

To this day, I walk onto the set of a television show, and I see fifty people looking back at me, waiting for me to perform. There's the production crew, the creative staff, the sponsors, and maybe an accountant or two—and they have a lot of time and energy riding on me. I have to go out and give my heart and soul in front of all these strangers. It can be pretty intimidating—and I just have to put those feelings and insecurities aside and do my thing.

And I still carry the voice of John Casablancas around in my head, saying, "By the way, Kim, you need to lose fifteen pounds." So I know what it's like to feel intimidated and inadequate—and I think that gives me something to say about the issues of self-esteem, self-respect, and self-confidence. It also gives me something to say about the issues of health and nutrition, because I learned that the ways I dealt with weight loss as a model—fad diets and starvation—were not healthy.

I didn't plan the course of my life. If I had, I would be standing behind a pharmacy counter right now—not writing a book. But I believe there is a loving God who makes plans for our lives that are far better than any plans we could dream up. I wanted to be a pharmacist; He wanted me to be a supermodel and a spokeswoman. I never could have planned the life that God has led me through. I can only conclude that there must be some reason He has given me a place of visibility in the media, and that He wants me to use this place to serve Him and to serve others.

So in this book I intend to talk about the issues I believe God has inspired me to talk about. Having been involved in the fashion world and the entertainment world, I have learned a lot about the evil and moral decay in the world—and I intend to talk about that in this book. Through the course of being not only a mother but a divorced and remarried mother,

I have learned a lot about what is really important in life, what holds families together, and what tears families apart—and I intend to talk about that too. Having discovered God, quite by surprise, some years ago, I have learned that the only true peace and joy to be found in this world come from a personal relationship with Him—and I'll be talking about that as well.

This is a practical, down-to-earth book, because that's the kind of person I am. It's also a deeply personal book, because I don't want to just lay out a lot of facts and ideas in these pages—I want us to really get acquainted. I hope you'll get to know me, and after you've read this book, I hope you'll drop me a note, in care of my publisher, and let me know how our chat together in these pages has affected your life.

This is not a political book, because I don't profess to be an expert on politics. But I think some of the experiences I've had as a model, a marathon runner, a media spokeswoman for health and nutrition, and a wife and mother have given me something to say about faith, family, and moral virtue. And those are the kinds of issues I'd like to talk over with you.

As I write these words, I'm thirty-eight years old. Some women would rather die than admit their age—but I'll tell you something: I'd rather be thirty-eight than be a twenty-year-old model again. I've come a long way, I've seen and experienced a lot of things. Some of what I know, I've learned the hard way. I've known people whose lives were destroyed by drugs and AIDS. I've been through the pain of a divorce. I've seen families ripped apart by the prevailing, destructive values of our times—and I've seen people and relationships healed by a rediscovery of the timeless truths of God. Out of all these varied experiences, God has given me a message—the message in this book.

Political activism, legislation, and involvement in the processes of our government all have their place—but the "model for a better future" I want to discuss with you is focused more on an internal change within each one of us than on writing laws and changing institutions. My "model for a better future" is about applying biblical Christian principles to our daily lives, and bringing about a change that works from the inside out rather than from the outside in. It's a change that starts within your heart and mine, then radiates out into the world through the authenticity of our lives.

Here are some of the issues we'll be talking about in the rest of this book:

- How to transcend the emptiness and superficiality of this world, so that you can be a person of genuine, lasting beauty

- Why faith in God is crucial to healthy homes and a healthy society

- How to build strong, healthy families in a world that is increasingly unhealthy and hostile to families

- How to maintain a healthy marriage

- How to live out our Christian faith in an anti-Christian world

- How to model and exemplify personal responsibility— and how to teach personal responsibility to our kids

- What we can do about abortion, teenage sex, and other social ills

- How to become personally, effectively involved in building a better future for our families and our society

All around us, we hear people demanding political or governmental solutions to the problems of our society. But the problems we face—racism, poverty, drugs, crime, teen sex, AIDS, and so on—are not political problems. They are individual problems, they are moral problems, they are spiritual problems—and those kinds of problems do not have political solutions. To change the moral climate of our society and solve the moral problems of our society, each of us must have a moral and spiritual change within.

New Challenges, New Adventures

In 1985 I did an underwater shoot for the 1986 *Sports Illustrated* swimsuit issue. Although I'm a swimmer, I was really out of my element and out of my comfort zone on that assignment. We were down in the Caribbean, and they got a bunch of us models together in a swimming pool (including my friend Kelly Emberg) and taught us to breathe underwater using scuba regulators. We had no masks or tanks. They would pull us down twenty feet and perch us on coral in our swimsuits. Then they would shove scuba regulators at us on poles, then take the regulators away and shoot the pictures. We'd be underwater for ninety minutes at a time, breathing only by gulps from the regulators.

I had very long hair at the time, and it kept floating around and getting caught in a coral branch. I tried hard not to panic, but I couldn't see well, and it was scary having to rely on other people for every breath while I kept getting snagged on the coral. At one point, while they were pulling me down deeper in the water to position me for another shot, it just got to me that I was twenty feet underwater and I had no control over the situation. I panicked, pulled myself free, and swam for the surface—probably kicking some people in the face in the process.

I got to the surface and climbed into the boat and began crying. Everybody was mad at me and yelling at me. I kept saying, "I don't want to go down there again!" But they kept telling me, "Come on, Kim, you have to! You have to grow up and do this!"

I realized they were right. My parents raised me to never be a quitter. They taught me that I should never quit for any reason other than sheer survival. I knew I had to go back down there and finish what I had started. It was a situation where I had to put my feelings aside and just do it, because I had made a commitment and people were counting on me. So I forced myself to do the thing I was afraid of. I went back down, finished the shoot—and I grew from the experience.

In the end, they hardly used any of the underwater shots we had worked so hard on. The models' skin came out looking blue, and that wasn't very attractive. They mostly used the abovewater shots, the beach shots, and the shots of Kelly and me on a salt mountain on the island. It was disappointing that we worked so hard on those shots and they were hardly even used—but I was still proud of what I had accomplished and what I had learned about myself. I discovered that I could face my fears and control my panic. I could push through those negative emotions and conquer them, and I could get the job done.

You only grow by taking on new challenges in life. You hold your breath and dive right in. More often than not, you find out the water is just fine. I really believe that God wants to use people who are willing to face their panic and fears. He wants us to jump right into the arena and boldly speak His message. He wants people who will stand at the crossroads of our society and make an unyielding stand for faith, family, and morality. He wants people who are willing to tackle new challenges and new adventures, despite their doubts, fears, and insecurities.

Remember, life is what happens to you while you're making other plans! So jump right in and join me! Let's talk. You and I are going to change the world together—

One life at a time.

2
My Journey

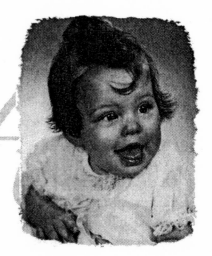

I was raised in the church. My mother, my younger sister, and I went every Sunday to a very old Presbyterian church—a beautiful, old, stone and stained glass church, built in the 1700s. The style of worship was very formal and straitlaced. When I was sixteen, I was elected a "youth elder" in the church. Along with all the businessmen and blue-haired ladies on the church board, they wanted two young voices—a teenage boy and a teenage girl—to contribute their ideas every now and then at the session meetings. It was a great experience, and I enjoyed being a part of the life of the church.

We had a great youth pastor named Ike when I was a high schooler, and I enjoyed the youth group activities. I was involved in the Interfaith group. We would make five and a half tons of peanut brittle every year, and we'd sell the peanut brittle to finance bus trips to Washington, D.C., or New York or Chicago. The trips were fun and educational, and we enjoyed some really great fellowship together, but I can't recall any deep spiritual benefit we received from these trips.

I enjoyed the youth group, but church itself was something I endured—much as my kids endure church now. I remember listening to the sermon, feeling sleepy or restless or fidgety. I was not able to understand what the minister was saying, or what God's Word was all about. As a child I sat in church for about half the service. Then all of the kids were dismissed to go to junior church. As I dashed out, I thought, *What a relief! I'm outta here!*

In church and in youth group, we had Bible readings. I was familiar with many of the stories in the Bible, and I had memorized a number of Bible verses. But to me, the Bible seemed almost impossible to grasp or apply to my daily life. I didn't know what it meant to have a personal relationship with Christ. I had never heard that such a thing was possible. No one ever asked me, "Have you accepted Jesus into your heart as your Lord and Savior?" No one ever said, "Kim, if you were to die right now, do you know for certain that you would go to heaven?" I called myself a Christian because I grew up in the church, attending every Sunday morning and every Wednesday after school, and I thought my good works and church attendance would get me to heaven.

"God Wants Me to Go Slowly With You"

When I was eighteen, I went to New York City and entered the modeling world. I got hit with so many new experiences in such a short time that I was really overwhelmed. In the process, I made some poor choices. Although I have no one but myself to blame for my choices, I realize now that my religious upbringing never gave me a spiritual basis for making all the right choices in life. At church, they never talked about morality; they didn't really apply God's Word to daily living. While I had grown up with the Bible and I knew a lot about the Bible, I didn't see how this Book was relevant to real life and real problems.

My parents taught me right from wrong, and they wanted me to live a moral life. To keep me pure, my dad promised me a new car if I remained a virgin until I finished college—and that was a powerful motivator! So I knew where I was supposed to walk, in a moral sense, but I didn't know how to do it. I didn't know God's Word very well, and I didn't understand that God's power to live a holy life was available to me through prayer and the Holy Spirit.

I got married in 1983 and my husband, Jim, and I had two children, James and Bobby. We lived in Florida, where we had a number of real estate investments, including several health clubs. Before we got married, I ignored a number of warning signs, including the opinions of several friends who thought I was making a mistake. After all, when you're "in love," no one can tell you anything. Over time, it became a difficult marriage, and we decided to separate in 1989, shortly after Bobby was born. I was planning to move back to New York City, so I told my husband, "I'll be busy with modeling assignments in New York, so I'm going to need a nanny. Could you put an ad in the newspaper?"

So Jim placed the ad, and this young woman, about twenty years old, came to our house. She had a bright, sunny personality, and she said, "Hi, I'm Ann Brown, and I'm here for the nanny position. I've packed my bags, they're in the car, and God told me I should work for you."

I thought, *God really talks to you? Right! I never heard about that in church!* But she had all the right qualifications, and I really believe that God put the thought in our heads: *Go ahead and hire her.* So my husband and I looked at each other and shrugged. "Okay, Ann," I said, "if God said you're to work for me, who am I to argue with that?" So we hired her. I told her that she would have to move to New York with me, and that was fine with her.

So the four of us—the two boys, Ann, and me—moved to New York. Except for visiting my parents in Buffalo at Christmas, we spent most of our time in a little two-bedroom apartment on the twenty-second floor in Manhattan. It was winter, so we spent a lot of time cooped up indoors—and Ann, bless her heart, used that time to work on me.

From October through December, she played her Christian music and read the Bible and talked about Jesus. Even though I had grown up with hymns and the Bible and talk about Jesus, this was different—and I didn't like it! I had never heard Christian music like this—it was praise songs, Maranatha music, and it made me want to clutch my ears and shut it out. It was like fingernails on the blackboard of my soul. Of course, I love all those songs today, and I listen to Christian radio constantly—but at that time, I could hardly stand it.

Sometimes Ann would talk to me about the Lord, but she was never pushy about it. Sometimes she would even seem to hold back, as if there was more she wanted to say, but it wasn't the right time. Several times she said to me, "God wants me to go slowly with you." And I thought, *That's strange! How does she know what God wants her to do? Does she hear a voice inside her head or what?* I didn't understand about the leading of the Holy Spirit.

I could see that her faith wasn't just a matter of going to church and doing religious things. It was a *relationship*—and in all the years I had gone to church, I had never experienced the kind of spiritual relationship I saw in Ann Brown. The more I saw of that special faith relationship in her, the more I wanted it myself. If Ann had tried to preach at me and push her beliefs on me, I probably would have rebelled. But the way she kept saying, "God wants me to go slowly with you," only served to pique my curiosity and my spiritual hunger. Instead of Ann coming to me and telling me that I needed Jesus in my life, I kept going to her when she was praying or singing or listening to Christian songs, and I'd ask her, "What are you doing? What is this all about?"

Sometimes Ann and the boys and I would be walking around the streets of New York, and we'd see a man begging in the street. Ann would walk right up to that man and say, "Oh, praise the Lord! Do you believe in Jesus?"

I would gasp and say, "Ann, don't talk to the panhandlers—and whatever you do, don't say 'Jesus' out loud on the streets of New York!" But I couldn't keep her from doing what the Lord told her to do. Sometimes the panhandlers and other strangers would swear at Ann and tell her to mind her own business, but she didn't care. She'd just skip on her merry way.

Ann Brown's Recipe for Heaven

Five or six years earlier, I had read a booklet on how to have a relationship with Christ. I had read the prayer in the booklet and made it the prayer of my heart and asked Jesus to come into my life. Though I was sincere at the time, my life didn't really change. But perhaps a "mustard seed" of faith was planted at that moment. Perhaps I truly accepted Jesus as my Savior then, but I just didn't understand what it meant for Him to be my Lord as well. In Mark 4, Jesus talks about a farmer planting seeds, which represented the gospel story. Some of the seed fell on rocky ground, some among thorns and weeds, and some onto good, fertile soil. At that point in my life, I guess the ground was a little rocky, and the gospel just didn't take root in my heart right then.

Even though God didn't have full control of my life during that period, I think He honored my prayer, protecting me from being fully corrupted by the world I was in. God eventually brought Ann Brown into my life to complete the process of my Christian conversion. I know that some people have an instantaneous, dramatic change in their lives when they first pray that prayer of commitment. Others, like me, are a little slow to get it. But every person is a unique individual, and God works in different ways with different people.

God used Ann's simple, quiet faith to stir up a hunger in me for a deeper and more real experience with God. Ann and I were in the apartment, talking together, and she said something about having the Holy Spirit living within you. "I want that," I said. "I want the Holy Spirit to live in me like He lives in you. How do I get that?"

After all those times of telling Ann to go slowly with me, I guess God finally told her to go ahead and spill it. "Well," she began, "you have to admit you're a sinner, ask Jesus into your heart, and renounce sin and Satan." She had a "recipe" for getting to heaven, and she began to tell me all about it. And it all made sense. I sure didn't want sin or Satan in my life anymore— and I really did want Jesus there. I questioned Ann about this "recipe" of hers. I wanted to make sure I didn't leave anything out—I wanted to get the "recipe" just right.

So after I was certain I had it down and wasn't leaving anything out, I prayed, and Ann prayed with me. Sitting in my little living room on the twenty-second floor on Sunday, January 21, 1990, I asked Jesus to take control of my life—to be not only my Savior, but my Lord as well.

I remember thinking, *Hmm! I don't feel any different.* I

thought that something should come over me like that cool breeze you're supposed to get when you eat a York Peppermint Patty. "Am I supposed to feel anything?" I asked.

"Don't worry about it," said Ann. "Jesus is living in you right now. If you're supposed to feel anything, it'll come."

And that made sense to me. I didn't doubt that my new faith was real. It had happened. I belonged to Jesus now.

Ann helped me find a church—the Times Square Church where David Wilkerson is the pastor. I still love to attend there whenever I'm in New York. Ann, the boys, and I would often go there on Sunday nights, and she would raise her hands, speak in tongues, and praise the Lord. Soon, I noticed my three year old, James, imitating Ann, raising his hands and saying, "Hallelujah! Hallelujah!"—though it sounded like "Ah-yah-yoo-yah!" After the service, we'd go home from church in the dark, at 10:30 at night in the middle of New York City. Some people would think we were taking a terrible risk, but we knew that no harm would come to us.

I still keep in touch with Ann Brown to this day. Just as she told me the day she answered our newspaper ad, God really did send her to me. That was her little mission that God gave her—to gently, quietly bring me to Christ. (Ann, if you're reading this, you did a good job!)

The Gentle Hockey Star

After my conversion experience, I went back to my husband in Jacksonville, Florida, and tried to make my marriage work. I really wanted the four of us to be a family again—a *Christian* family. More than anything in the world, I wanted my boys to grow up in a loving, healthy, intact Christian family.

I attended Ann's church in Florida. To make sure I had

received the Holy Spirit, there was a laying on of hands (as described in Acts 8:17; 1 Timothy 4:14; and elsewhere in Scripture). As my Christian brothers and sisters laid hands on me, I experienced the feelings I had asked Ann about before— only it wasn't like a minty cool breeze from a York Peppermint Patty. It was a hot fire, like the tongues of fire described in Acts 2:3. I felt the power of the Holy Spirit come down on me.

Jim and I tried to make a go of our marriage, but we were unable to salvage it. In September of 1991 we separated again— this time for good. After counseling with pastors and other spiritually mature Christians, I reluctantly came to the conclusion that there were biblical grounds for divorce in our situation. So I went back to New York City to think and pray about the future.

For a number of years I had been traveling back and forth, maintaining an apartment in New York and a home with Jim in Florida. My career had come to a standstill. I considered studying acting and voice in New York and taking my career in a new direction. I spent four days alone in my apartment. I prayed, I listened to Christian music, I read my Bible, and I listened for the leading of the Holy Spirit. I wanted to know if my career plans were God's will—or just my own.

At the end of those four days, I was convinced that I should move to New York for good. I began house-hunting, using a real estate agent recommended by my girlfriend, model Carol Alt. She was married to the New York Rangers hockey star Ron Greschner, and the real estate agent she recommended handled most of the real estate transactions for the players on the Rangers team. I met with the agent and told her I was looking for a house to rent in Connecticut. It happened that she was trying to sell a house owned by a Rangers forward named Ron Duguay.

Not being much of a hockey fan, I didn't realize that Ron Duguay was one of the most popular, fan-pleasing, high-scoring players on the team. The fans loved his daring offensive play and his long, flowing hair. The real estate agent thought that the two of us should get together, so she told me about Ron—and she also told Ron about me.

It happened that Ron was appearing in an ad around that time, and the company needed a female model to appear in the ad with him. Remembering what the real estate agent had told him about me, he said, "What about Kim Alexis?" He thought that working with me in the ad would be a great way to meet me. The advertising people said, "Well, she'd be terrific—if we can get her."

Long story short—they got me.

So I went to the shoot for this ad, and that's where I met Ron Duguay. It was a Sunday, and I took my boys to church that morning at Times Square. After church, the boys, their new nanny (not Ann Brown—she was off helping others), and I all went to the location for the shoot. At one point, the photographer was getting some single shots of me, so I was busy. I thought the nanny was looking after James and Bobby, but she was sitting and talking to somebody, and not paying close attention to the boys. Sure enough, one of my boys picked that time to wander over toward a big, sparkling fountain.

Ron saw what was going on, and he followed my son, keeping a close eye on him to make sure he wouldn't fall in the fountain or hurt himself. When I looked and saw Ron standing there by the fountain, watching out for my son, I was impressed. Hockey players have a reputation for being rough, aggressive players in a violent sport. But this man was kind, thoughtful, and gentle. From that moment on, I just wanted to touch him—to touch his hand, his face, his back. I think it was his strength combined with his gentleness and caring that touched me—that's a very husbandly, fatherly combination. Ron didn't even know I was watching him—but he immediately won my heart.

So that was our first "date."

"You Have to Be Born Again"

Soon after that, in 1992, Ron's friend Phil Esposito, who used to play alongside him and coach him with the Rangers, called Ron down to Florida to try out for the Tampa Bay Lightning, a new expansion franchise in the National Hockey League. Phil was president, general manager, and part owner of the Lightning, and he believed Ron's flamboyant, crowd-pleasing style would help ignite the Tampa Bay fans and get the Lightning off to a rousing start.

For Ron, who was thirty-five at the time, Tampa Bay would be his chance for a comeback—a last chance to get back into the NHL. He went down to Lakewood for training camp, and even though he had been a star during his years in New York, he now had to prove himself to get on the team. Ron is a quiet, reserved guy who likes his own space, and he didn't feel like hanging out in the hotel with the rookies. Instead, he commuted ninety minutes each way between his home and training camp, and as he drove, he listened to Christian radio stations. (This was the Bible Belt, and there were plenty of such stations to listen to!)

He was struggling with injuries and was coming to the end of his NHL career. Ever since he was a kid, all he wanted to do was play hockey. He had realized his dream, becoming one of the stars of the game—but now that dream was coming to an end. I think the loss of that dream made him all the more receptive as he listened to the music and teaching on Christian radio. One night, as he was driving, the radio Bible teacher he was listening to gave an invitation to accept Jesus as Lord and Savior. And there, on that road, Ron gave his life to Christ.

Ron and I were dating at the time, but he didn't say anything to me about the decision he had made. Like I said, he's a *very* quiet guy! By this time, the divorce decree from my first marriage had been issued, but it was still taking months to sort out my finances from those of my first husband. Ron was also divorced, with two children of his own. I knew that I had really fallen in love with Ron, and I was thinking of him as the man I wanted to spend the rest of my life with.

Just a few days after Ron committed his life to Christ, he got hurt and was cut from the roster of the Tampa Bay Lightning. His NHL career was over. That was in October of 1992.

On November 15, 1992, Ron sat me down and asked me to marry him. It was everything I wanted—but was it what God wanted? I had to know. "I want to marry you," I said, "but I can't give you an answer until we have prayed about it."

Though I didn't know Ron had committed his life to Christ at that point, we had prayed together many times before. So that night, we went down on our knees together and we prayed, "Lord, if this is what You want us to do, please let us know. And if You don't want us to be married, please make it clear to us. Show us Your will, because we don't want to do anything that isn't Your will—and neither of us wants to go through the misery of a divorce again!"

We continued talking after we prayed, and I said to him, "You know, I had decided that if I was ever going to get married again, I would marry a preacher."

"A preacher!" Ron exclaimed. There was a look of panic in

his eyes, as if he was thinking, *I could never be a preacher!* "Why would you want to marry a preacher?" he asked.

"My first marriage was so painful for me and my kids," I said. "I don't want to be hurt like that again. I figure if I could marry a preacher, I'd be marrying someone who would always stay close to God, and he could help me stay close to God. Besides, if I were married to a preacher, I could be more involved in the church, and I think I'd like that—the life of a preacher's wife."

"Well," he said, "I hope you're not stuck on this preacher thing, because I could never do that."

"No," I said, "you don't have to be a preacher. That's just an idea I had. But I'll tell you what you *do* have to be."

"What's that?"

"You have to be born again. I will not marry you if you are not a born-again Christian."

He looked at me strangely. "What do you mean, Kim? What is that? What does 'born again' mean?"

I said, "You have to accept Jesus into your heart."

"Oh," he replied, "okay. You tell me what I have to do to be born again, and I'll do it."

He still didn't tell me he had previously made a commitment to Jesus Christ while listening to the radio in his car. Though he was already born again, though his commitment to Christ was real, I don't think he quite knew how to label what he had done—but whatever it meant to be "born again," he wanted to make sure he did it. He didn't want to leave out a step.

I called Ann Brown, and I said, "Ann, I need your recipe for being born again. My boyfriend, Ron, wants to marry me, but I told him I can't marry him unless he's born again."

So Ann gave me the recipe again, just as she had that day in my apartment when I turned my life over to Jesus Christ. I wrote it all down, making sure I got everything she said. Then I showed it to Ron, and we got down on our knees together and went through the prayer of salvation, step-by-step. And Ron asked Jesus into his heart—for the second time, I later found out. But that's okay—the Lord doesn't mind being invited again and again. He just wants to know that the welcome mat of our hearts is always out for Him.

Ron and I were married in Tampa, Florida, on January 2, 1993. He has become not only my husband and my lover, but also my prayer partner, my business partner, my counselor, my coach, my soulmate.

Baby Steps to God

I look back on my early Christian life—my babyhood as a believer—and I realize I made a lot of mistakes. Some were mistakes of ignorance, because I just didn't know very much about how to apply the Bible to my daily life. Others were mistakes of spiritual immaturity, because maturity as a Christian is a lot like physical maturity. It doesn't happen to you all at once—*boom!* It's a growth process—slow and sometimes a little painful.

The good news is that God is a very patient, loving, understanding Father, and He knows that we are often like spiritual toddlers. We don't know where the dangers and perils of life are, and sometimes (just like my little boy, that first day I met Ron) we wander over by the fountain, without any conception of what might happen to us if we fall in. But God—this strong yet gentle Father of ours—is very watchful and loving. Just as Ron followed my little boy and watched over him while I was busy with the photographer, God followed me around through my Christian babyhood, keeping a protective eye on me, giving me my freedom, but always ready to tug me gently back from danger if I ventured too close.

Change Begins Within

You may be wondering what being "born again" has to do with making the world a better place. Simply this: You cannot change the world until you change the people who make up the world—beginning with you and me. All change begins within.

Most people don't understand that. They try to change the world by changing laws, by coming up with government programs, by electing certain people to office, by carrying signs and demonstrating or going on strike. I'm not saying it's wrong to do those things. I'm saying that if you think you can solve the world's problems through government programs or education or legislation, then you are completely missing the point. Those are all external fixes. They don't fix the problem *within*—the sin problem that is inside every one of us.

What are the problems we face in our world today? Injustice and inequality, racism, crime, war, political corruption, pollution, domestic violence, broken families, single parent families, teen pregnancy, child abuse, drug abuse, and on and on. Every one of these global problems is rooted in the universal human problem: sin. As a society of individuals, we are lost, we are out of alignment with the will of God—and all the suffering we see around us is the result.

As long as you and I, as individuals, remain lost, stuck in our own sin, we cannot be part of the solution. We can only be part of the problem.

So it all starts with you and me, in the privacy of our own hearts. This is the only life you and I will ever have—we won't get it back later, so we dare not waste it. We have to begin living lives that matter, lives that are worthy of God. And we have to begin sharing our own stories with the people around us, so that they, too, can begin to deal with the problem within.

Once we have stopped being part of the problem, we become part of the solution. And once we have become part of the solution—then what?

Well, turn the page with me and let's think about that together . . .

3
*Living Healthy
in an Unhealthy
World*

When I was a model in New York City, I would come home after work and make myself a big bowl of fresh fruit for dinner. I was living alone—this was before I was married and had children—and I would kick back, click on the TV, and put my fork into a big, juicy bite of fresh apple or papaya. Just as I was bringing that bite of God's healthy food to my mouth, a commercial would come on the screen. It might show a juicy, sizzling, fat-laden hamburger with greasy fries and sugary soft drink, or maybe a pizza loaded with salami and pepperoni and artery-clogging cholesterol! And I wanted it! I wanted to race out of my apartment and get a pizza with everything on it or a Super-Size Monster Burger Combo to go!

That's the world we live in—a world that constantly pressures us and our children to make unhealthy choices. It's not easy to live healthy and eat healthy in an unhealthy world. Every day, with every choice we make, we are either moving toward health or away from health. We are never in a static condition. The state of our health does not, as some people seem to think, just stand in one place. Nor are we doomed to simply become less and less healthy as we age.

Every meal, every morsel of food we consume, either elevates or lowers the state of our health. Even if we are getting on in years, even if we are overweight or have a chronic health condition, there are things we can do to move in the direction of greater health. Once we realize that truth, once we are aware that the state of our health is largely in our own hands, we can begin to make the choices that lead us to healthier, happier, more effective lives.

Is it really so important that we live healthy lives? You bet it is! The level of your health is critically important to your ability to function as a parent, as a partner in your marriage, and as the person God wants you to be in the world. I know that I'm happier as a human being and more effective as a wife and mother if I am eating right, exercising appropriately, and getting a sufficient amount of rest. There's no better way to get up in the morning than to jump out of bed knowing you've had a good night's sleep and you have no reason to feel guilty about anything you ate or drank the previous day.

Good health is not just a physical issue. It's a moral and spiritual issue as well. We should not, as some people do, discount the importance of physical health, saying that the human body is not important compared with the human spirit. In His Word, God makes it clear that both the body and the spirit are important, because both belong to Him: "Do you not know that you are the temple of God and that the Spirit of God dwells in you? . . . Therefore glorify God in your body and in your spirit, which are God's."[1]

I'm not suggesting that we should become obsessed with our bodies, with being unnaturally thin or exercising to the point of being muscle-bound. I'm suggesting that we all need to find God's *balance* in life. People who are obsessed with avoiding food and weight gain are frequently either anorexic or bulimic. These are serious, even life-threatening eating disorders, and they should be treated by medical professionals.

But in my life, I've met very few people who are anorexic or bulimic. It is much more common in my experience to see people whose eating disorder is in the opposite direction—they are chubby, overweight, or downright fat! They don't eat to live, they live to eat! And compulsive overeating is just as much an eating disorder as obsessive anorexia or bulimia. Unhealthy eating habits threaten this body, this temple of God's Spirit that He has temporarily entrusted to our care. We need to find that healthy balance—that spiritual, godly balance—between caring too much about eating and simply being careless about our eating.

Living Healthy on the Go

We all live busy lives, and we all have to eat. People often say, "I don't have time to fix healthy food! I'm on the go! I have to grab what I can—and I often have to let my kids fend for themselves! I don't have time for anything else!"

Okay, let's stop the excuses. Healthy living is a crucial priority, so let's treat it that way. Since we all have to eat, that means we all have to go to the grocery store and to restaurants. Why should it take any more time to make a healthy choice than an unhealthy choice? You know, it doesn't take any more time to toss a salad, slice some whole wheat bread, and broil four salmon steaks than it does to microwave four TV dinners!

It doesn't take more time to make healthy choices for ourselves and our families—it just takes more thought. It can be as simple as knowing what to choose from the restaurant menu or knowing what foods to pack in our children's lunchboxes. We are what we eat. If we take unhealthy food, unhealthy music, or unhealthy entertainment into ourselves, we will become physically, spiritually, morally unhealthy people. If we feed ourselves on God's good, natural food, on God's Word, and on godly music and entertainment, we will become the kind of strong, active, effective people God intended us to be.

Some people expect me to be a fanatic about nutritional matters, thinking I must eat only vegetarian or that I avoid all fat or some such thing. Actually, I eat a lot of meat, including red meat. I don't weigh my food by the ounce or consult tables of calories or grams of fat. I just try to maintain a balance, and I try to keep it natural. In my eating habits and in food preparation for my family, I tend to focus more on principles than on details and calorie-counting. In general, the principles I follow are:

- Eat lots of fruits and vegetables.

- Eat foods that are high in protein.

- Eat whole grains, not white.

- Avoid added salt, sugar, or chemical agents such as colorings and preservatives.

- Avoid added fat, but don't get too obsessed with naturally occurring fat in foods (our bodies need *some* fat). For example, I don't avoid a good trimmed but marbled steak; I go ahead and eat dark-meat chicken but not the skin; I eat meat that is grilled, not fried (because frying adds fat); I have salad dressing (in moderation) on my salads because undressed greens are just not that appealing to me; our family also eats lots of raw nuts, which contain a high amount of naturally occurring fat, but are also high in protein.

- Whenever possible, eat organic, natural foods. The word *organic* is a very specific term, referring to fruits and vegetables produced without synthetic fertilizers or pesticides (the soil must be free of synthetic additives for at least three years), and to meats and dairy products that are free from chemical injections or additives, such as antibiotics or hormones.

If you eat out a lot, you know that most restaurants today cater to a health-conscious clientele, featuring menu offerings that meet all of the criteria I list above. You may have some special health condition or chronic problem that limits your diet, but even so, you can usually find healthy foods that meet your special needs in most restaurants.

In recent years, I've discovered that wheat gluten and I just don't get along, so when I go out to a restaurant, I may order a lean, grilled hamburger patty without the wheat roll, or I'll have a piece of grilled fish or salad with meat in it. If you don't have a problem with gluten, you'll be glad to know that many restaurants now serve brown rice and whole wheat bread and pasta.

Our family's diet contains a fair amount of fat—maybe 25 percent fat versus protein and carbohydrates—but no one in our family is fat. We don't obsess with eating foods that are labeled "less fat" or "fat-free." I think a lot of people are finding that a lot of so-called "fat-free" processed foods are filled with extra sugar to compensate for the taste that is lost when the fat is removed. Oftentimes, "less fat" and "fat-free" foods simply taste terrible and are unsatisfying. I would much rather have a little naturally occurring fat in my diet and be satisfied than eat something labeled "fat-free," with an ingredient list that reads like a chemistry book and tastes like something out of a test tube.

In our family, we simply make sure we eat foods that are high in protein, along with a lot of vegetables and fruit (which ensures that we get plenty of fiber). We enjoy the wholesome, natural foods we eat—though, as you may expect, my kids have been known to complain about our meals being too wholesome. Still, I know I'm doing the right thing for my kids, and I push on!

Understand, what works for me and my family may not work for you and yours. You may be a vegetarian and say, "Oh, I wouldn't touch meat!" You may want to get your protein from tofu, eggs, cheese, yogurt, fish, beans, whole grain pastas and breads, or soy burgers—that's fine! I would simply suggest that you try to achieve a balance of natural, simple foods, and foods high in protein and fiber but low in added fat and artificial yuck.

Though I don't eat bread and pasta anymore (because I can't tolerate the wheat gluten), I used to make homemade whole wheat pasta and breads with my children. Those times spent making food with the children build irreplaceable family memories, and the children just love to help. With the bread- and pasta-making machines that are available today, it's easy and inexpensive to make wholesome, fresh bread and pasta. You feel proud of yourself when you make your own natural food at home, you demonstrate good nutritional values and habits to your children, and the foods you make at home really do taste better!

For high protein and low fat, consider varying your family's diet by adding game meat, such as buffalo, venison, rabbit, ostrich, or emu. And before you ask—no, buffalo is not an endangered species anymore, and yes, these meats are more expensive than chicken and beef. But they are more widely available than you may realize. You will need to check the freezer section of your supermarket or go to a specialty store, but these healthy, high-protein, low-fat meats are available across the country. Frequently, if you tell your supermarket butcher that you'll buy buffalo or ostrich meat, he will be happy to special order it for you. And just look at how these meats compare with chicken and beef:

100 gram serving of:	CALORIES	PROTEIN in grams	FAT in grams	CHOLESTEROL in milligrams
Chicken	239	18.2	17.9	83
Beef	214	31.0	31.0	92
Buffalo	180	35.6	1.4	40
Ostrich	106	21.7	3.0	36
Rabbit	143	20.5	8.2	57
Venison	159	25.0	3.3	66

So it's clear that game meats offer a much healthier option— higher in protein and lower in fat and cholesterol than beef and chicken. This is not to suggest you should avoid beef or chicken—we certainly eat our share in the Duguay household. I'm only suggesting that you might want to add a little extra-healthy variety to the main dishes on your family's table from time to time. And if more people would go to their grocer or butcher and ask for such things as organic vegetables and buffalo meat, the grocery stores would begin supplying this demand, and the prices of these items would eventually come down.

The Importance of Enzymes

One way my husband and I get our family off to a healthy start each morning is with fresh vegetable juice. We have our own juicer, and the juice we make is better than anything that comes in a can. I'm not knocking V-8 juice, but how can any canned juice beat what we make at home? We take tomatoes, fresh parsley, romaine, garlic, cucumbers, celery, and carrots, push them through the juicer, and start our day with juice that is incredibly delicious, with no added salt, and with all the precious nutritional enzymes completely intact. (Our kids help make the juice too—boys just love to shove things into machines!)

Enzymes are an important and often-overlooked part of balanced nutrition. They are proteins produced by living organisms that help regulate the chemical reactions in the life cycles of living things. Some enzymes release energy to regulate our heartbeat and breathing, while other enzymes help us to digest and utilize our food for energy, growth, and body functioning. Very tiny amounts of enzymes are used to regulate and stimulate the high levels of physical and mental activity our bodies produce. So it's important that we have enzymes in our diets.

The problem is that when food is processed, it tends to lose its natural enzymes. Heat processing, whether in cooking or pasteurizing, is deadly to enzymes. And juices, when allowed to sit for more than four days, also lose their enzymes. So fresh fruits, vegetables, and juices are far preferable to canned or bottled products. That's why an orange is much better for you than a glass of bottled, pasteurized orange juice—you get more of the benefit God put in the orange, including the enzymes and the fruit fiber.

If your body does not get enough enzymes from the food you eat, then the body must draw from its own strength to digest your food. This is a nutritional consideration for both adults and for children. When Noah, my youngest, was six months old, I stopped breast-feeding him. I didn't want to put him on pasteurized baby formula, so we fed him fresh, raw goat's milk. We chose goat's milk over cow's milk because goats have far fewer diseases than cows, and we chose raw milk over pasteurized milk to make sure that the natural enzymes were still in the milk.

Two general rules I follow when I'm shopping for my family are:

1. Shop the outer aisles of the store.

2. Look for "God's packaging."

The natural, unprocessed foods tend to be in the outer aisles, around the perimeter of the store. That's where the produce aisles, the meat cases, and the dairy cases are. The middle of the store is reserved for the food that has been canned, bottled, boxed, processed, dyed, and generally turned into something the body has trouble recognizing as food. Looking for "God's packaging" means looking for apples and berries instead of Fruit Roll-Ups and Fruit Loops.

Sometimes I don't even go to the grocery store. I just go to the local produce stand or farmer's market to buy fruits and veggies. You have to seek out such places—but when you come home with those bags of real food in God's packaging, you feel better. When you serve it to your family, your family feels better. You treat your own body, and the bodies of your family, as the temples of God's Spirit that they truly are.

Keep Kids Happy with Healthy Substitutions

Sometimes, when I'm standing in the checkout line at the grocery store, the clerk will ask, "Do you have pet rabbits at your house?"

"No," I say. "Why?"

"Well, all those fresh vegetables in your cart! Nobody buys that many vegetables unless they have some kind of animal to feed!"

Now, isn't that amazing? People expect us to feed animals better than we feed ourselves and our children! If we want to raise healthy children in this unhealthy world, we need to make responsible, healthy choices at the grocery store.

I recently bought a lunchbox for my youngest son to take to school. I opened it, and there were packages of candy inside. Instead of a Thermos bottle, there was a space to hold a can of soda pop. It's just expected nowadays that kids will grow up consuming candy and soda every day. Whatever happened to drinking pure water?

Understand, my kids are no different from anyone else's. They see commercials, they walk past vending machines and candy counters, they have friends who eat all this stuff. If I let them, they would eat all this sugary, gunky, artificially flavored, chemically colored junk food too! That's to be expected. They're kids! But we are the grown-ups, we're the parents, and we have a God-given responsibility to stand between our kids and an unhealthy society that is trying to push all this stuff down our kids' throats.

I don't enjoy saying no to my kids, so I try to find creative ways to say yes. Kids like fizzy, bubbly drinks, and that's fine. I won't give my kids Coke or Surge or Mountain Dew, but I will tell them, "If you like bubbles in your drink, you can have some club soda. If you want a little flavor, we'll add a splash of fruit juice or a squeeze of lemon juice. But you don't need all that sugar and caffeine and artificial color." A lot of parents don't realize how much phosphorus there is in soda pop, or that phosphorus causes kidney stones. The kidneys can't filter out all the phosphorus, so it collects and turns into stones, which can become a very painful problem. Also, many experts believe that aluminum soda cans could add toxic amounts of aluminum to our diets; researchers have found a possible link between Alzheimer's disease and aluminum deposits in the brain.

When I take my kids out to McDonalds, I tell the person at the counter, "Just water or orange juice to drink, please." They say, "But the soda comes with the Happy Meal—it's free!" And I have to politely say, "But I don't want it. I want the water or orange juice."

Sure, it's easier to say yes to our kids all the time; it's easier to make unhealthy choices. We live in a world that is structured to offer unhealthy choices to our kids at every turn. But our job as parents is to teach them how to live healthy, even in an unhealthy world.

Understand, we don't have a completely ascetic lifestyle. Our family enjoys an occasional trip to the ice cream parlor, where we enjoy ourselves over a luscious ice cream sundae. But ice cream is an occasional treat. We don't keep cartons of ice cream in the family freezer. Since they don't have ice cream all the time, I think they appreciate it more on those occasions when we go out to the ice cream parlor.

Packing healthy lunches for kids can be a challenge. I make their sandwiches with whole wheat bread—but my youngest doesn't like bread, so I just roll up turkey or chicken for him and put it in a sealable plastic bag. I try to give them apples, grapes, oranges, carrot sticks, or celery sticks, and a bottle of juice or water for school. For crunch, I'll give them crackers or potato chips—yes, I know, the fat in the chips is not great, but if you keep the sandwiches low in fat (light on the mayo!), a little fat from the vegetable oil in the chips won't hurt.

What about birthdays? Shouldn't kids be able to have sweets

and cake and ice cream at a birthday party? Well, yes—and no. Yes, kids should have birthday cakes on their birthdays—but does that mean it has to be a bakery cake made out of processed junk, smothered in powdered sugar and Crisco? Why has cake-baking become such a lost art among mothers today?

And I don't mean baking a cake from a Betty Crocker box, either! For my children's birthdays, I make my own pound cake or butter cake with fresh organic butter and eggs, and raw cane sugar (not refined) and whole wheat flour (not white). I whip it all together, and it's absolutely fabulous—just ask my boys! I top it with a fluffy cream cheese frosting, sweetened with real maple syrup, and my boys gobble it up.

But the other kids? A lot of them push it away. Not because it isn't tasty, but because it's not what they expect from a birth-day cake—pure white, airy cake coated in sugary, greasy frost-ing. These kids have lost their taste for what's real and good and natural.

Children should be mostly flat in front—they should not have little round, protruding tummies. My kids are muscular and lean, and their tummies are hard, not soft and jiggly like the tummies of a lot of their peers. My middle son, Bobby, has a sweet tooth, and for all my efforts to keep him on a healthy diet, he does manage to get his hands on sweets from time to time.

One summer day, Bobby came to me, pointed to his shirt-less tummy, and said, "Mommy, I think I'm getting too much of a belly on me—what should I do?"

Ron was standing nearby and said, "That's easy. Stop eating cookies, and eat more protein and veggies."

Well, Ron has the flattest set of stomach muscles you ever saw—so when Bobby got advice from a real NHL star with the flattest abs in town, he listened!

My children go to a private Christian school. When the

school opened a snack shop as a fund-raiser, all the kids started buying ice cream and chewy candies called Airheads. When I found out about it, I went to the school office and talked to the administrators of the school. After that, the snack shop offered fresh fruit and yogurt (yes, the yogurt has sugary jam in it, but it's better for kids than Airheads).

It's up to us, as parents, to take responsibility for our children's health. Children can't be blamed for liking sweets and not liking spinach salad. They can't be blamed for not worrying about health consequences. Their job is to experience, play, grow, and explore. Our job is to protect them, provide for them, and train them to make good choices as they mature.

It's natural and normal for kids to say, "Yuck! I don't want that! I want candy!" The attitude of a child is, "If it doesn't feel good, I'm not doing it! If it doesn't taste sweet, I'm not eating it!" That's an immature attitude, and immaturity is the normal state of a child. But our job is to guide our children from a place of making immature choices to a place of making healthy choices. It's part of our spiritual and moral obligation as parents.

I see kids out at a restaurant with their parents, and they order a Shirley Temple or a virgin piña colada. Kids think it's cool to get an adult-looking beverage in an adult-looking glass, just like Mom's and Dad's. But what message does that send to our kids? Doesn't that promote the idea that drinking is cool? That being a grown-up means getting to have a drink at the bar? That's not a message I want to impart to my children.

All too many parents—including, sadly, many Christian parents—are neglecting to teach their children how to make good choices. If the kids want it, the parents give it to them. It's easy, because they can afford to give their kids everything they want, and it's easier than setting rules and sticking to those rules. But in doing so, these parents fail their children and allow them to slip into the clutches of this unhealthy, instant-gratification culture we live in. I think it's very sad—and a little scary—that so many parents today are abdicating that basic parental responsibility.

I can understand why so many parents have simply given up. They know that their kids are living in a way that's not healthy, but they are simply too exhausted to fight the battle anymore. All the other parents in the neighborhood buy the sugar-sprinkled, neon-colored goop their kids see on the commercials, and it just becomes too difficult to swim upstream against the culture.

But we have to take a stand. We have to tell our kids, "No more! I'm not buying you any more food that glows in the dark! I'm not buying you any more food in which the first three ingredients are sugar, sugar, and sugar. Yes, you're going to see commercials and vending machines and shelves full of that stuff. You're going to see your friends eating that stuff. But this is *our* family, this is *your* future, and we are taking a stand for the sake of your health."

Our job is to set an example for our kids and to explain to them why we make an effort to provide them with healthy food. We should tell them that if they build healthy eating habits now, as they grow older, they will avoid weight problems and have more energy and better health. They'll be able to avoid the pimples and skin problems that sugar-addicted, junk-eating friends will face.

Shut Down the Noise

Our culture is bent on tilting our children's tastes and cravings toward every imaginable extreme. Our kids are being taught that life is supposed to be an unending succession of thrill-ride, theme-park experiences. Every sport has to be an extreme sport, or it isn't any fun. Every pizza must "go to the edge," no boring crust. Ice cream can't be just a sundae or a shake any-more—it has to be a McFlurry or a Cappuccino Blast. It's not enough that Fruit Loops are sugar-coated and neon-colored—they now have to be Marshmallow-Blasted Fruit Loops. Every-thing kids eat has to be some kind of Mega-Monster-Mighty-Morphin experience to the Max!

Why does breakfast have to look and sound like a video arcade game? Whatever happened to normal, natural foods? When kids are eating stuff that practically strobes, how can we ever hope to interest them in foods like apples and oranges and bananas? It's tough, but that's our challenge as parents. We have to sell them on God's natural foods in God's natural packaging.

In nutrition, just as in matters of morality and spirituality, we have to parent against the culture. We have to teach our children not to be sucked in by the seductive messages of the world. Nobody said it would be easy. Fact is, it's very hard—but that's our job as parents.

Our children are surrounded by noise and stimulation all day long. God says, "Get rid of the noise. Shut down the stimu-lation. Be still and know that I am God." So I try to feed my children the things that are natural and wholesome and edify-ing to their minds, their spirits, and their bodies. In addition to feeding them good, natural food in God's packaging, I feed their spirits on good, wholesome music that points their thoughts toward God. I play Christian worship music on the CD players in their rooms at night—it plays softly as they're going to sleep, and continues playing all through the night. When they wake up in the morning, it's the first thing they hear. They love it, and they get up in a great mood.

I don't make a big distinction between spiritual, moral, emotional, and physical health. These are all just different dimensions of one human being. If we would see the task of parenting as one of nurturing and feeding our children what they need to grow in *every* dimension of their lives, then the challenge of feeding their bodies would just fall right into place.

It's important that our kids hear the same message from us, no matter whether the issue is what they watch, what they read, what they listen to, or what they eat: "I know you'd rather have something else, but I'm feeding you something better, something good and natural, because I love you. That's why I give you healthy music to listen to, healthy books to read, and healthy food for your body. I love you too much to let you put just anything into your soul and into your body."

Gentle, Natural Exercise

I'm an athlete, and I've run seven marathons (that's right, real marathons—26.2 miles each!). I used to subject myself to a very intense, strenuous, rigorous exercise program. But I can't do that anymore. I don't run marathons these days. I still exercise—but in a gentle, natural way, not in the extreme way I once did.

I mentioned in a previous chapter that I have a thyroid condition, and it is largely that condition that has affected the way I exercise. My doctor has told me that the excessive and strenuous way I used to exercise has damaged my endocrine system—the system of glands (thyroid, adrenal, and pituitary) that produce hormones that pass directly into the bloodstream. The stress of my thyroid disease, coupled with the stress I put on my body, had caused damage to my adrenal glands, which produce hormones that help the body adapt to stress.

I realized that I had a problem because I was becoming fatigued a lot. Every time I exercised, I would gain about three pounds of water weight and I would get exhausted—not just normally tired, but flat-out exhausted. The doctor told me that after years of strenuous exercise, running marathons after having babies, flying all over the country in my career, and just being a mother, I was burning my candle at both ends. In short, I had burned out my adrenal glands.

The doctor told me I was at a very critical point (I was thirty-seven at the time). "If you don't take it easy and totally stop everything," she said, "you're going to do irreparable damage to your body." That was very unusual advice she was giving me, because she usually had to tell her patients to exercise and be more active. But she knew me, the fast pace I was keeping, and the strenuous exercise I was doing—and she knew I was overdoing it.

"You need to practice moderation even in exercise," she said. "You need to stop and let your adrenals and your thyroid build up again. Give your body a chance to regather its strength and heal itself."

That was the first time I had ever heard that there was such a thing as "too much exercise." It's something you never hear about because all too few of us are in any danger of reaching that point. But I had reached it—and here's why:

The 1980s were the era of "high-impact aerobics" and strenuous exercise. If you weren't sweating and straining over an hour a day, you weren't really working out. That was the era when I really got into physical conditioning and running marathons.

Then came the 1990s. "High-impact aerobics" gave way to "low-impact aerobics." Soon, doctors were telling us that instead of long, hard runs, we should take gentle walks and swim, because all the high-impact exercise of the 1980s had stressed out our ankles and knees. So now we're joining water aerobics classes and taking up crewing (rowing), because these are low-impact activities that elevate your heart rate without damaging your joints.

In the 1980s I was spending an hour a day on the Stairmaster, with the resistance cranked up full-blast, thinking that I was really exercising. Not anymore. Today, I do my stretching exercises in bed and I play with my kids in the pool and I walk—and that's enough exercise for me. After burning out my adrenals, after overstressing my body, I'm gently working my way back into a sensible, moderate exercise program. I've strengthened my adrenals by taking supplements, and I'm on the right thyroid medication—and I'm getting stronger.

So I take a different approach to exercise from the one I took ten years ago. Just as I believe in eating naturally, I now believe in exercising naturally. Everyone should do at least twenty minutes of good, brisk walking every day. That doesn't mean you need to go to a gym or that you need to put a treadmill machine in your family room. You have a neighborhood, don't you? Then take twenty minutes a day to walk through it and wave to your neighbors! You have errands to do, don't you? Well, next time you're out doing errands, find ways to incorporate exercise into your trip. Instead of circling the parking lot until you find the closest space to the door, park at the end of the lot and walk. Instead of taking the elevator or escalator, take the stairs.

We like to exercise as a family—it's a great way to have quality time together and do something good for our bodies at the same time. Our pastor once asked families in the church to do a "spiritual fast," abstaining for one month from television, and replacing the tube with healthy substitutes such as Bible study and family activities. When we unplugged the TV, we found lots of extra time for sitting and talking, watching sunsets, playing board games, going fishing or golfing, swimming in the pool, taking walks in the neighborhood or on the beach, or roller-blading. In the cool of the evening, Ron would go out on the nearby golf course and hit a few balls, and the boys and I would strap on our blades and go skating along the cart paths until we found him.

I didn't tell the boys, "Let's get some exercise, it'll be good for us"—that would spoil it! I just said, "Let's go have some fun!"

I believe it's important for parents and children to exercise together. Kids need to see that their parents care enough about their own health and their children's health to continue to be involved in healthy physical activities. Children and young people feel indestructible, as if their health is permanent, it'll always be there and never go away. I felt that way when I was younger, and most young people do. As parents, we need to teach our children that our health is not to be taken for granted—it must be nurtured and protected or it will be lost.

When you get to be my age—in your late thirties, heading for forty—you become aware that you are losing an edge you once had. You're not feeling the same as you did when you were twenty. You wake up and realize that the same amount of yardwork, housework, exercise, or tennis that you used to breeze through a few years ago starts to wear you down today. You can't skip a meal or lose a few hours of sleep as you used to.

Once, one of my boys came in from the pool with a sunburn. He had used sunblock, but either he didn't apply enough or it came off in the pool. In any case, his face was red from the sun. When I mentioned it to him, he shrugged as if it were no big deal. I said, "You know, that sun damage on your face can never be completely repaired. There are cells in your skin that were damaged and they will always be damaged—there's nothing you can do to fix it. And if you keep on damaging your skin that way, you'll end up with old, wrinkled skin."

His eyes got big and he said, "What?! I hate that!"

He realized something important about his health, and he's been much more careful about his sun exposure ever since. When kids are young, they don't realize that they can never get back what they had the day before—unless we tell them. It's up to us to teach our children and model for our children what it means to live healthy in an unhealthy world. It means making choices between what seems good at the moment and what is *really* good for us. It means feeding our minds and our bodies on the right kind of food. It means getting out and exercising in a way that stretches our muscles and gets our heart surging, but without straining ourselves to the point of harm.

Every choice we make—even the choice of whether we eat that cookie or take those stairs—is a choice that either moves us toward or away from better health. The choices we make are moral and spiritual choices. Every moment of our lives, we are choosing whether we will tear down this temple God has given us—or build it up and cherish it. Let's glorify God in our bodies and our spirits, which belong not to us but to Him!

4

Genuine Beauty in a Superficial World

A magazine interviewer once asked me, "How does it feel to be a sex symbol?"

I laughed! "I'm not a sex symbol," I said.

"Get off it!" the reporter insisted. "Of course you're a sex symbol! You've done six *Sports Illustrated* swimsuit issues! You've done *Vogue* and all these other magazines! How can you tell me you're not a sex symbol?"

"But I really don't feel I've ever been a sex symbol," I said. "I'm an athlete, I'm a wife and mother, I'm a woman, but I'm not a sex symbol. I'm not in this business because I want to generate lust in men! That makes me uncomfortable! I've always hated it if I felt a certain photo of me might be used to arouse lust in men. I never set out to do that, and I've never viewed myself as a sex symbol."

I don't want to be attractive to a lot of men. Every day, I pray as a wife, "Lord, let me be attractive to my husband, let me do what's appealing to him." He's the only man I want to please.

What Message Are We Sending?

When I go out in public, I represent Christ, and I dress accordingly. I see many women, including many Christian women, who dress in such a way that makes you wonder whom or what they represent! They go out in public—and even go to church!— dressed in a way that is tantamount to indecent exposure, with cleavage down to *here* and a skirt hiked up to *there*. It's worse than distasteful. It's dishonoring to God.

Don't we have enough focus on superficial beauty in our media and in the world around us? Do we have to bring this kind of erotic superficiality into the church?

I believe that God wants His people to make themselves as beautiful as possible—but the beauty He desires is not only a physical beauty, but a beauty of spirit, a beauty of modesty, a beauty that goes deeper than the surface of the skin.

One test I wish these women would apply to themselves: If Jesus walked into the room, would they be glad to see Him—or would they blush with shame?

Or consider this question: Say you're on a lonely road, your car has broken down, and you're dressed in a sexy little low-cut top and a skirt that's hiked right up to your underwear. Some men approach you—and it's not clear what they have in mind. Do they want to help you? Or take advantage of you? Would you feel exposed and vulnerable—or would you feel safe? And would the way you are dressed affect how secure you feel?

I believe many women are playing with fire in the way they dress. Understand, if a man does anything inappropriate toward another woman, regardless of how she's dressed, he's 100 percent responsible for his actions. He's completely in the wrong.

'ery small comfort to a woman who has been
iken advantage of or hit on in some way. The fact
itting out the message "I'm available" by the way
she d... hen she is responsible for putting herself in a compromising position. Dressing modestly tells the world, "I respect myself and I insist on being treated with respect." Dressing like a floozy tells the world, "Look at me, want me, lust after me. I'm easy and you can have me." Displaying intimate parts of the body is a form of advertising for sex—so if you dress to attract sexual attention, you can hardly blame anyone else if that kind of attention comes your way.

Your clothes are a form of self-expression, a personal statement—about as personal a statement as you can make. You are speaking to the world with your body. You are sending a message about your values, your moral standards, and your intentions. As a child of God, a daughter of Christ, I constantly try to remember the message my Lord would want people to receive from my appearance.

Fix the Inside

People often turn to me for beauty tips, but that's not really what I do. Most of the time, I go around with my hair in a ponytail and no makeup on. It's a natural way to be, and I'm happier that way. I try to focus my attention on the beauty within, on making my soul and spirit pleasing to God and to others.

To me, the first, last, and best beauty tip is this: Try to see yourself as others see you. Having a sensible, moral mind-set is much more important than having a chic, worldly fashion sense. It is possible to dress modestly without looking like the schoolmarm from *Little House on the Prairie*. It's possible to be stylish and attractive without wearing something that is too short, low-cut, or see-through.

I've also been asked what I think of cosmetic surgery—breast augmentation, face-lifts, tummy tucks, and so forth. My standard reply has gotten me in a lot of trouble, but I continue to stand by it: "I'd never pay someone to cut me with a knife." I said that when I was in my twenties, at the height of my modeling career—and I caught a lot of flack for it!

Newspaper and TV reporters called and practically bawled me out. "What do you mean?" they demanded. "How can you say that? You're in your twenties now, and that's easy for you to say. But when you get to be fifty, you'll want your tight, youthful skin again."

"Look," I said, "when I'm fifty, I'll wear my wrinkles as a badge of honor. I think wrinkles are proof that you've lived and earned your way in the world. They're a sign of character." Well, I'm older now, and I've started to get those wrinkles, all right—but my views haven't changed. I still want them to keep that knife away from me!

Is cosmetic surgery ever a valid choice? Yes—in the case of a mastectomy or a serious burn or a physical deformity. I believe in *corrective* cosmetic surgery, but I would never have *elective* cosmetic surgery. If you're considering having something lifted, tucked, reduced, or enlarged in order to become more physically perfect, my advice to you is simple: *Save your money.*

Instead of having some doctor cut into your body, focus on accepting yourself as you are, as God made you. If you can change your physical appearance by becoming more healthy, by exercising more, eating less, and burning off excess weight—great! But if I had $10,000 to spend on cosmetic surgery, I'd much rather give it to the poor than give it to some Beverly Hills plastic surgeon.

Do you want to feel better about yourself? Fine. Fix the problem inside first, and then you won't even need to fix the outside. Give the money to God or to the poor instead of lavishing it on your own vanity—then you'll truly feel better. Believe me, if you only fix the outside, you might just ruin your life. There are many women who have felt inadequate because of a small bust, so they have gotten breast augmentation surgery! Now they have the big superstructure they always wanted—and they have to go out and flaunt it! They have to show everyone their brand-new extra-large bust! It has even led some women into immorality and the loss of their marriage.

The problem is that when you only fix the outside and don't deal with the obsession inside, you haven't really changed anything. The obsession is still there, and it's still driving your behavior. Before, you were obsessed with feelings of inadequacy. Now, after the surgery, you are still obsessed—you are obsessed with letting everybody see your beautiful new body! You have to run to Victoria's Secret and buy out the store! In the end, you are just as obsessed and unhappy as you were before. You've got a new set of breasts, and some rich doctor has a new sailboat—but you still haven't fixed the inside, only the outside.

Why change what God has given you? I probably have the smallest breasts around—so I'm speaking from experience. (I was larger before I breast-fed three baby boys—they took all I had and then some!) It's not as if I can't get by with what I have—I can and I do. I just don't think God wants me to implant plastic bags of silicone gel in this body He gave me. If God had wanted me bigger there, He would have made me bigger. He didn't, so I'm going to leave well enough alone. I think I'm happier as a woman and an athlete with small rather than extra-large.

The apostle Paul talked about a "thorn in the flesh" he had, some physical problem or limitation in his life that kept him humble. God told Paul, "I'm going to leave that physical limitation in your life, because it forces you to rely on Me." That makes a lot of sense. Perhaps God keeps me humble by making me what He wants me to be. I really don't want to mess with that—I want to simply be what He made me to be, so that He can use me as He intends.

Try Something New!

A friend once asked me, "What should I do with my hair? It's all frizzy, and I just don't know what to do with it!"

I looked at her hair a moment, then said, "Pull your bangs back."

She looked in a mirror and pulled her bangs back—then she started laughing hysterically. "Oh, no!" she said, "look at me! That's awful! I can't go out with my forehead bare like that!"

I looked at her again and said, "What's wrong with that? I think it's fine."

She gasped. "Oh, I could never go out without my bangs!"

"Well, what about a black-tie affair?" I asked. "You wouldn't wear bangs to a formal dinner, would you?"

"I'd have to! I can't go anywhere without my bangs!"

I hear these attitudes all the time: Women who have absolutely rigid, inflexible rules about what they will or will not do with their hair, makeup, clothes, and so forth. My advice to such women: Get over it! Try something new! Don't get stuck on one look, one hairstyle, one way of doing your makeup.

We models know how important it is to try new looks, new styles, new approaches. Every day, we go to a different modeling assignment and someone gives us a different opinion:

"Let's do this with your face. Your hair's all wrong, let's do it this way. We'll have to do something to hide that part of your body." That's why most models don't have specific opinions about how their hair should be done or how their makeup should be applied. We have been accepted and told we're beautiful and photographed in every conceivable permutation of hair, eyes, lips, makeup, and on and on and on.

That's why models inevitably get to the point where we just want to wear jeans and a T-shirt in our off-hours. That's why we reach a point where we say, "You fuss! I'm not fussing with me!" We just can't imagine doing our hair or our nails or our makeup, because other people have been doing them all day. Many times, by the end of the day, I didn't even want to touch my own face because it was sore from everybody else messing with it. I didn't want to brush my own hair, because my scalp was tired.

One day they'd put my hair up, the next day they'd want it flowing down my shoulders, and the day after that it might be in curls. They might put me in a beautiful mink coat, or a swimsuit, or a jogging suit, or an evening gown—and no matter what they did to me, they'd tell me, "Beautiful! Gorgeous! Wonderful!" Obviously, I couldn't afford to get locked into one look, one style—and neither should you.

Experiment. Try something new. Try something different.

This is particularly hard advice for many mature women to take—women in their fifties or sixties or so. I know many mature women who have a set image of themselves in their minds and they're not willing to change it. Their makeup has to be the same every day (even the same brand), their hair has to be the same style from week to week (and has to be done by the same beautician)—everything must be the same, never any changes.

Sometimes I feel a little embarrassed for these women who think they need to have those long eyebrows drawn onto their faces with pencils, and who put these hysterical-looking colors around their eyes. They haven't changed their hairstyle, their hair color, their eye makeup, their lipstick, or anything else in twenty, thirty, or forty years. I want to *gently* say to them, "Maybe—just maybe—it's time for a change. It's okay to try a new look. You might even feel better about yourself."

If you try something and it doesn't work, you say, "Okay, now I know that particular look doesn't work for me." And you try something else. Even models find that some looks just don't work for them. You simply work around it. You find your best features and you work with what's good.

Contrary to what many people think, models aren't physically perfect. No one is perfect. We all have flaws. We are all aware of features we don't like. Believe me, we models are the first to know our flaws, the first to hide them—and we dwell on them constantly.

All models have insecurities. Even if we get paid millions of dollars to be photographed, even if people are constantly telling us, "You're beautiful! You're the best!"—we know our flaws, we're painfully aware of them, and we are horribly insecure about them. There's not a model in the business who doesn't feel that way—not one. We all wake up every morning, look in the mirror, and wince at that flaw, that thorn in our flesh.

And I'll tell you something else that all women do—and yes, I mean *all women,* including supermodels: We all look for the flaws in other women, especially those women who seem "too perfect." If we can find any little imperfection in that supermodel or that beauty contestant or that woman who just flirted with our husband, then we can feel a little better. And don't tell me you don't do that! I know, because I do it too!

That's why I keep coming back to the profound truth that the beauty we should focus on is *inner beauty,* not surface beauty. On the outside, we are aging, we are losing our youth and our beauty day by day. But if we are focused on inner beauty, we can actually become more beautiful with each passing day. We can become more patient, more gentle, more compassionate, more strong, more truthful, more devoted, more gracious, more faithful, more Christlike with every new day.

That's why, when I think of women I've known who are truly beautiful, I tend to think more of saintly, wise, wonderful women whose images would never be found on the cover of *Vogue.* They are women who may have little remaining of the youthful outer beauty they had in their twenties—but they have acquired a depth of beauty that I truly want to have when I'm their age.

Over the years, I've been observing many of the older women in my life, searching for mature role models I could look up to, learn from, model myself after—women who really have it together spiritually, morally, intellectually, athletically, and nutritionally; women who have kept their vows and have loving husbands and godly children to show for it.

I don't know of any *one* woman who has *all* those qualities, but I have met a number of wonderful women who exhibit many such qualities. I've watched them, and I've seen how they relate to their family and others. I've watched how they deal with the empty nest and with grown sons, because I want to be prepared when that time comes for me.

Women like that are my model for a better future.

Because sooner or later, like it or not, I'm going to be where those women are today. I'm not a young supermodel anymore. Already, I'm getting those little lines when I smile. And true, those little lines are not that much fun to look at.

But let's "face it" (ha ha!), I'm a mature woman and I'm a mother, and I think I have to grow gracefully and say to the world that there's more to Kim Alexis Duguay than my looks. I am not defined by my superficial, outer appearance. I am defined by what I do, what I say, what I believe, and what I exemplify. The real Kim is right here, inside of me—

And the inside of me is growing closer to Christ every day.

5

Staying Pure in a Polluted World

Two days after my eighteenth birthday, I arrived in New York City, signed a contract with John Casablancas and the Elite agency, and entered the modeling world. Two days after that, I landed my first professional assignment. The Elite agency sent me to Rome to be photographed for a *very* big Italian magazine—one of the biggest.

I was checking into the hotel in Rome when I saw a girl running through the lobby. She was one of the European models for the magazine shoot. She was barefoot and wore a filmy white dress, with no underwear, no bra. I was horrified! My mother had taught me to dress up when traveling. In fact, I had flown all night across the Atlantic attired in a dress, panty hose, and high heels. I had my small-town, upstate morality about me—and here was a casual display of near-nudity in a hotel lobby, something I had never encountered before.

Next, I met with the people who explained to me what the job would entail. There were other models around the magazine office, and they were from all over—America, England,

France, Italy. Some had obviously been in the business awhile and knew their way around. We were all chatting or gossiping with one another. One of them said to me, "They're looking for a model to appear on the cover, and you have just the right look. Of course, you have to do a little extra to get a cover."

"A little extra what?" I asked. There was a point I was supposed to get—but I wasn't getting it.

The other models shook their heads at the poor innocent from upstate New York. "Darling," one of them said, "most of the girls who get on the cover have to sleep with the owner of the magazine."

"Oh!"

Now, you're not going to believe this, but it's absolutely true: When they told me that, my reaction was, *What? I don't have to do that, do I? What do they mean—"sleep with him"?* I was so naive, I thought they literally meant *sleep*. I mean, I knew what sex was, but I didn't know it was called "sleeping" with someone. I would have been totally aghast if I had realized what they *really* meant!

The people at the magazine made me work all day long, then all night long. It was an incredibly busy time because all the designers were presenting their new haute couture lines to the press and public. I worked around the clock, since I had to be available for the different photographers. I was constantly changing clothes, showing different lines and different collections.

Being a kid from Lockport, fresh out of high school, I had no idea what a big deal it was to wear all those designer clothes. Other models would have killed for the chance—but me? I didn't know the difference! I thought some of the clothes I modeled were absolutely fabulous—but there were some outfits I wore that I thought were absolutely hideous! I didn't know what fashion was, what beauty was. All I knew was that these people made me work long hours, and I was incredibly tired.

When I finished shooting in Rome, they put me on an early-morning plane to Paris. I was put up in a room with a girl who worked for the magazine executive. Her boss was the guy I was supposed to "sleep" with. He was in the next room, on the other side of an interconnecting door.

When I got to the room, I was so exhausted I instantly dropped into the bed and fell asleep. Apparently, as I slept, the girl conveniently left the room. The next thing I knew, I was awakened by the magazine executive. He spoke only Italian, and I didn't know what he was saying to me. Finally, in broken English, he said, "Can I get you anything?"

I looked at him with eyes that could barely focus and said, "No!" And I went back to sleep.

A few minutes later, he woke me again and said, "Can I get you anything?"

Again I said, "No!" and went back to sleep. He did that three or four times, and I was so stupid I really didn't know what he wanted.

Finally, just to get him to stop bothering me, I said, "Okay, could you get me a glass of water?" So he got me a glass of water, I drank it, and went back to sleep. He didn't bother me again.

Living in a Polluted World

There were a lot of sexually predatory men in the world I traveled in, but I wasn't bothered by them very much. I think men on the make have a sixth sense about women. They know which women are vulnerable to their advances, and which won't put up with their nonsense.

There is an image of the model's life being a glamorous whirlwind of travel, exotic photo shoots, parties, excitement, and men. Well, sometimes that's true. But for me, the life of a model consisted mostly of being alone in an endless succession of shoebox rooms in horrid little European hotels, no TV or room service, nothing for company or entertainment but a good book (I spent far more time with my nose in a book than I did at parties). My life consisted of trying to find a decent place to eat, exchanging currency and figuring out a foreign language, and trying to stay happy enough so that the misery didn't show through my eyes (you can't hide it).

I saw a lot of destructive, immoral behavior in the fashion world. During the 1980s, a lot of models used cocaine or smoked joints (lately, heroin has become the drug of choice). I think people do drugs largely because they want to fit in, or (in the case of cocaine) they want to stay thin, or they are simply bored. Being an athlete, I didn't want to pollute my body—the thought of filling my lungs with smoke or putting chemicals in my bloodstream made me ill.

When I was in New York, I liked to go to Studio 54 to dance. I enjoyed the excitement and the music and the motion. A lot of people, though, went there to score. Looking back, I think I didn't really understand all the things that were going on around me. In my small-town, upstate way, I was very naive about a lot of the sex, drugs, and other destructive things people did—and that's fine with me. I'd just as soon be stupid when it comes to such things.

I'm not saying I was perfect—far from it! God was not a big part of my life at that time, and I made some choices I'm not proud of. But when I think of all the evil and destructive behavior that surrounded me, I'm grateful that I avoided the more dangerous temptations.

On one of the TV shows I worked on recently, the cast and crew stayed in a hotel on location. Long after midnight, I could hear talking and laughing and carrying on in the halls. I later learned that people had been partying and carousing from room to room, and there was a lot of outrageous, immoral behavior going on. By that time in my career, I had gained a reputation as a Christian—a "goody two-shoes"—so I wasn't invited to the goings-on. In fact, people would hide this kind of activity from me, because they knew I had strong opinions on moral issues.

Immorality is all around us. We live in a morally polluted world. This pollution is found not only in the fashion world or the entertainment world, but in your world, in your neighborhood. The pollution comes into your home through your TV set, your radio, your morning newspaper and magazines, and your computer. The pollution is lapping at your doorstep. If you do not protect yourself, it will seep into your mind and pollute your soul.

Of course, those most threatened by the current tidal wave of moral pollution are our kids. They are being lied to by the media and even their schools. They are told that values and virtue and morality have no place in the world anymore. They are told that it is impossible to live a life of purity and abstinence, and that the only thing that matters is that the sex they engage in be "safe." They are not being told that the only "safe sex" is sex that waits until marriage.

Many educators claim that the reason kids engage in risky sex is that they have not received enough information. But if you talk to today's young people about sex, you'll soon find out that they have plenty of information. They know where babies come from. They know what condoms are for. They know how AIDS is transmitted. They know the mechanics of sex. They don't lack information. They lack wisdom, values, and a moral basis for right behavior.

One of the biggest problems with sex education programs today is that the information they dispense is partial and misleading. Kids are taught that condoms offer "safety" in sex, even though condoms are known to have a 20 percent failure rate. I ask you: Would you consider airline travel safe if one in every five flights ended in a crash? Hardly. Why, then, do we allow educators (aided and abetted by condom manufacturers, who are reaping the profits) to sell our kids on the notion that "latex sex" is "safe"?

Suppose, for a moment, that condoms actually do protect against AIDS as advertised (they don't, but let's pretend they do). Is anyone out there bothering to inform our kids that condoms provide little or no protection whatsoever against other diseases, such as herpes, the human papillomavirus, and chlamydia? According to the *New England Journal of Medicine,* 20 percent of all American adults have genital herpes—a chronic, incurable disease—and 90 percent of them don't even know it! And since the 1970s, cases of genital herpes have risen 500 percent among teenagers.[1] So much for "safe sex."

Christian teens are hardly immune from temptation. In fact, they are in almost as much peril as the general population when it comes to sexual experimentation. According to a survey conducted by the Josh McDowell Ministry, 43 percent of the fourteen hundred churchgoing young people who were questioned responded that they had engaged in sexual intercourse by age eighteen.

No society in the history of humanity has ever been as awash in moral pollution as America is today. That is why Dr. Billy Graham warns, "If God withholds judgment from America, He will owe Sodom and Gomorra an apology." People in the fashion capitals of New York, Rome, and Paris are having affairs and acting out degrading fantasies—but so are people in Small Town, U.S.A., so are people in churches all over the country. If you are looking to fulfill your most depraved fantasies, you can do that any place in America. But if you want to find God and His fulfillment, you have to turn your back on the pollution of this world, and you have to seek God and His righteousness.

God's will on this matter is absolute; it's black and white. As Paul writes in 1 Corinthians 6:18, "Flee sexual immorality" (NKJV). Flee it. Run from it. Get as far away from it as you can. Cancel the R-rated cable TV channel you find so tempting. Block those Internet sites from your computer. Don't put yourself in situations of temptation or compromise. Find a close friend or two that you can trust and ask them to hold you accountable for the absolute purity of your thoughts and behavior.

Our first priority is to purify our inner selves. Only then can we see clearly enough to hold the rest of society accountable for morality and purity. Jesus put it this way:

> Why do you look at the speck of sawdust in your brother's eye and pay no attention to the plank in your own eye? How can you say to your brother, "Let me take the speck out of your eye," when all the time there is a plank in your own eye? You hypocrite, first take the plank out of your own eye, and then you will see clearly to remove the speck from your brother's eye.[2]

Jesus is saying, "Start within. Remove the immorality, hatred, lust, and greed from your own life first. Take the lumber out of your own eyes. Only then do you have the right to tell the world that it can't see straight."

It's Never Too Late to Wait

Okay, you and I are clear on the fact that we have a big problem. But what does God say about this problem?

I think we sometimes have a hard time hearing God's voice when it comes to matters of morality, because the voice of the world is so loud, it drowns out the still, small voice of the Spirit. So we wander through our lives in darkness, never taking these issues very seriously. We have bought into the false ideology of our enemy. Without even going to God and finding out what He has to say on the matter, we have compromised His truth and surrendered in the war for spiritual and moral purity.

Some people today say, "I don't need religion to be a moral person. I define my own morality." That is arrogance. That is a prescription for moral anarchy. If everybody defines his own morality, there are no standards at all. The only standard of morality becomes, "This is what I want to do, and no one can tell me not to." That's absurd! The very definition of *morality* is "a commonly accepted system or standard of right and wrong conduct." So if anyone says, "I am a moral person, but I refuse to recognize any limits on my sexual expression," we have to call that person on it. If someone wants to live without any behavioral boundaries, that's up to him. My answer to that is, "What you do in private is your business—but don't call yourself a moral person. Just be honest enough to admit that you are an immoral person, doing immoral acts."

I am not the Kim Alexis Thought Police and Judgment Co., but I do have a responsibility before God to speak the truth in love. And the truth of God regarding moral behavior and moral standards is found in His Word. After all, God created sex—it's His gift to the human race, to be shared within the protective enclosure of a committed marriage relationship.[3] If we want to use that gift in a healthy way, then we need to read the "instruction book" that came with that gift.

From the Bible, we learn that God created both men and women in His image,[4] but because of the entrance of sin into the world, the image of God has become distorted. As a result, God's gift of sex has been horribly abused and misused by men and women.[5] The Bible speaks very frankly and clearly about what God considers a misuse of our sexuality, including adultery,[6] incest,[7] prostitution,[8] indecent exposure,[9] homosexual behavior,[10] and even lustful thoughts and viewing pornography.[11]

God has given us rules of sexual morality not because He wants to ruin our fun, but because He wants the very best for us—the deepest, richest, most joyful sexual experience possible! Because of His wonderful love for us, He tells us in His Word:

Now the body is not for sexual immorality but for the Lord, and the Lord for the body. And God both raised up the Lord and will also raise us up by His power. Do you not know that your bodies are members of Christ? Shall I then take the members of Christ and make them members of a harlot? Certainly not! Or do you not know that he who is joined to a harlot is one body with her? For "the two," He says, "shall become one flesh." But he who is joined to the Lord is one spirit with Him.

Flee sexual immorality. Every sin that a man does is outside the body, but he who commits sexual immorality sins against his own body. Or do you not know that your body is the temple of the Holy Spirit who is in you, whom you have from God, and you are not your own? For you were bought at a price; therefore glorify God in your body and in your spirit, which are God's.[12]

Here, God warns us through the apostle Paul to *flee* premarital and extramarital sex—not because God is mean, rigid, and controlling, but because He wants the best for us. He wants us to be whole and healthy in body, mind, and spirit. He wants us to be sexually pure not only so that we can avoid sexually transmitted diseases, but so that we can enjoy healthy, stable, fulfilling marriage and family relationships. Sex is His gift to us, and He has given us His guidelines so that we can enjoy the gift of sex as it was meant to be enjoyed.

The message we hear all the time in the media is that the greatest sexual satisfaction is found outside of the boundaries of marriage. The facts prove otherwise. Statistical studies have shown that couples who marry after a trial period of unmarried cohabitation (sometimes called a "trial marriage" or just plain "shacking up") have a much higher divorce rate than those who marry in the traditional committed way. University of Wisconsin researchers found that 38 percent of shack-up-first couples divorced before reaching the ten-year mark, compared with 27 percent of those who marry as virgins, the way God intended.

And let me be candid with you: My experience fits those statistics. Though my church and my parents told me that I should be a virgin when I married, no one really explained to me why virginity before marriage is important. I didn't understand the biblical reasons for chastity, and the fact that God designed His moral laws for good, practical, loving reasons. He established His moral laws so that children would be born into the safety and security of healthy, stable families—not the chaos and insecurity of shack-up and divorced relationships. Jim and I lived in a "trial marriage" before we made it legal, and true to the statistics, we split up a few years later, creating a time of upheaval and insecurity in the lives of our two boys.

Studies also show that religious faith, values, and moral standards contribute to sexual satisfaction, and "very religious women" report greater satisfaction in sexual intercourse with their husbands than "moderately religious" and "non-religious women."[13] So biblical morality, which says that sexual expression is reserved only for marriage, is truly designed to enhance our relationships and to make our sex lives more meaningful, joyful, and satisfying.

The Bible offers a much different view of marriage from that of the world around us. Marriage is a very special union—what the Bible calls a "one-flesh" relationship, as Jesus Himself said:

> And He answered and said to them, "Have you not read that He who made them at the beginning 'made them male and female,' and said, 'For this reason a man shall leave his father and mother and be joined to his wife, and the two shall become one flesh'?"[14]

I'm sure you know the common, vulgar terms people use to describe the act of sexual intercourse—blunt, offensive four-letter words that could just as easily describe the mating of two alley cats in heat. But the Bible uses an elevated and beautiful word to describe sexual intercourse in marriage—a word that describes sexual intercourse as a union of deep intimacy. That word is *know*. In the Bible, a husband and wife don't just have intercourse with each other—they *know* each other, they exchange an intimacy that goes beyond the body, beyond the mind and emotions, all the way to something deeply spiritual and beautiful. Sex is an extension of all the many dimensions of their one-flesh intimacy together, as we see in Genesis 4:1: "Now Adam *knew* Eve his wife, and she conceived . . ." (NKJV, emphasis added).

Within that protective enclosure of marital intimacy, the Bible tells us that two people who truly *know* each other and are committed to each other in a covenant of marriage can explore the full range of mutual pleasure that sex allows:

> Let your fountain be blessed,
> And rejoice with the wife of your youth.
> As a loving deer and a graceful doe,
> Let her breasts satisfy you at all times;
> And always be enraptured with her love.[15]

Our polluted world tells us that cheap sex is fun, wholesome, and the way to intimacy and fulfillment. Wrong. Within marriage, sex is a healthy expression of intimacy. Apart from marriage, sex is usually a selfish guy exploiting a desperate girl. She's so eager to connect with another human being, to be "loved," that she's willing to settle for the fake intimacy of cheap sex. If that desperate girl is *you,* then please listen: Don't fall for his smooth talk and his easy promises. Hold out for real intimacy with someone who loves you enough to prove it with a legal, holy commitment. Don't sell yourself short.

Marriage isn't just a "piece of paper," as people so often say these days. Marriage is proof of commitment. The person who says, "Our love doesn't need a piece of paper to prove it's real," is a person who already has the back door open and his sneakers laced up. Don't be fooled. Hold out for that all-important "piece of paper." It spells *commitment,* and you're worth the wait.

I know waiting isn't easy. It takes strength, character, and faith—the faith to believe that God knows what He's talking about in His Word, the faith to live in obedience to God even while our feelings and our hormones are screaming, "I want it!"

The world says, "Everybody's doing it." God says, "Let 'everybody' else be wrong. You do what's right." What's more, "everybody" is not doing it. More and more, Christians are recognizing the need for purity and patience. Even if you've blown it in the past, you can choose today, starting right now, to live as a virgin again. It's never too late to wait for marriage.

We all want to live in a clean society, free of the moral pollution that has infected our media, our government, our workplaces, our schools, our neighborhoods, and even our churches. It's good to become involved with decency groups that fight pornography on a local and national level. It's important that we involve ourselves in our kids' education and know what they are being exposed to in the schools. It's important that we talk to our children and make sure they understand God's view of sex and morality.

But as important as all those actions are, our first priority is to purify ourselves within. That means replacing impure thoughts with pure thoughts. As my favorite passage of the Bible says:

> Finally, brethren, whatever things are true, whatever things are noble, whatever things are just, whatever things are pure, whatever things are lovely, whatever things are of good report, if there is any virtue and if there is anything praiseworthy—meditate on these things. The things which you learned and received and heard and saw in me, these do, and the God of peace will be with you.[16]

Change must begin within you and me. We must stop *polluting* our minds and begin *feeding* our souls with pure food. We feed the soul by actively, aggressively thinking on the things that are pure and true, and especially by basking in the pure truth of the Word of God. When we do that, God promises that His peace will be with us—Wow!

Facing the Truth

Do you remember Donna Rice? In 1987 her name was linked to a sex scandal involving presidential candidate Gary Hart. The candidate's presidential hopes were destroyed when photos of Senator Hart and Donna Rice, taken in Bimini in the Bahamas, were published in the *National Enquirer.* But there's a lot more to the story than most people realize.

Raised in Georgia and South Carolina, Donna Rice faithfully attended church and Sunday school as a child. She made a decision to commit her life to Christ when she was in the ninth grade. Donna was active in her youth group and church choir, went on mission trips, and often brought school friends and neighborhood friends to church. She wanted other kids to know about Jesus Christ, just as she did. How, then, did this good Christian girl get caught up in a sordid media scandal?

In an interview with *Today's Christian Woman* magazine, she explained that, after high school and college, she began drifting away from her Christian friends and the morality she was raised in. "I began to compromise my Christian values—partying and dating guys who weren't Christians. I told myself, 'We won't get serious, so it won't hurt anybody . . .' Eventually, I, like many of my Christian friends who had backslidden from their faith early in college, stopped attending church and reading my Bible. That summer I also began to date an older guy. One night, after a few drinks, he forced me to have sex. I was so ashamed that I didn't tell anyone."

That experience of date rape was a catastrophic turning point in her life. She fell even farther away from the Lord. "I was devastated," she said. "I'd wanted to give my virginity to my husband on our wedding night, so losing it against my will was horrible. I kept thinking, *It's all my fault.*" The man who raped her later called and said that he didn't realize that she was a virgin or that her "no" really meant *no*—he thought she was just playing a game of hard-to-get. This, of course, is part of the "rape myth" promoted in our society, particularly in pornography.

After that experience, Donna tried to escape the pain and shame of the rape. She entered (and won) a beauty pageant, and worked as an actress and model in New York and Miami. In the entertainment world, she fell even farther from the faith she was raised in, and began dating a drug dealer who often cheated on her. She left him, but her self-respect was so diminished that she kept returning to him. Though she felt God tugging at her heart, she would not let go of her lifestyle. She did not want to change.

After her boyfriend was sent to prison, Donna was introduced to Senator Hart at a political fund-raiser in Miami in March of 1987. The senator asked for her phone number, and the next day he invited her to dinner. The day after that, Senator Hart, Donna, and another man and woman cruised to Bimini aboard the *Monkey Business,* returning the following day. The senator, she confessed, "swept me off my feet." Before they returned to Miami, Senator Hart told Donna that he was going to run for president. Afterward, he called her a number of times, telling her he wanted to keep seeing her, but he could not leave his wife. Donna was left to wonder about her feelings for him, and his feelings for her.

One night, she turned on the TV and began watching the Franco Zefferelli movie, *Jesus of Nazareth.* Instantly, she was convicted by God over how far she had strayed from His plan for her life. She decided to meet the senator one last time and tell him their brief affair was over. She didn't know that the other woman on the boat was apparently peddling photos from the Bimini trip—photos of Gary Hart and Donna Rice together—to the newspapers. When she arrived for the meeting with Senator Hart, reporters had the meeting place staked out.

On May 3, 1987, the story came out in the *Miami Herald*. Shortly afterward, the Bimini pictures appeared in the *National Enquirer*. Hart's candidacy was shredded—and so was Donna's reputation.

For months after the scandal broke, she was hounded by the media. "I was offered millions of dollars to talk," she recalls. "It was hard to turn down the money since I didn't have a job, but I didn't want to exploit my notoriety because I knew the way I'd been living was wrong . . . My mom and grandmother urged me, 'Donna, before you make any decisions, get your life straight with God.' I was stunned because I hadn't yet realized I could put the entire mess in His hands."

Around the same time, a girlfriend from her church youth group days sent Donna a tape-recorded message. "Donna," she said, "I imagine you're in a lot of pain right now. I just want you to know that God loves you and I love you." On the tape, the girlfriend also sang some songs that she and Donna had sung in church together years before—and Donna fell to her knees in her apartment and wept. "I knew I—and no one else—was responsible for my choices. I cried out, *God, it took falling on my rear in front of the whole world to get my attention. Help me to live my life Your way!* God answered my plea by flooding me with His presence and forgiveness and by surrounding me with Christian fellowship."

Almost ten years after her life was nearly destroyed, Donna Rice is back in the spotlight—but now she is on the right side of morality, fighting against moral pollution instead of being drawn into the vortex of scandal. Now married to businessman Jack Hughes, Donna Rice Hughes is the national spokeswoman for Enough Is Enough!, a nonprofit organization that seeks to end illegal pornography and make the Internet safe for children. She has also written a book on protecting children from Internet porn, *Kids Online: Protecting Your Children in Cyberspace* (Fleming H. Revell, 1998). Since I am a board member of Enough Is Enough!, I'm very proud of Donna and the work she's doing.

It's hard to imagine how painful it would be to have your secrets splattered across the newspaper headlines, as happened in Donna's life. But she would be the first to tell you that there is a moral principle at work in the world, and we cannot ignore it: "For there is nothing covered that will not be revealed," says Luke 12:2, "nor hidden that will not be known" (NKJV). Yet God is gracious. He has taken Donna's past and transformed it into a blessing.[17]

We serve a holy God, a God of love and of moral absolutes. That is not a contradiction. His moral laws are a direct result of His love. He loves us too much to allow us to continue harming ourselves with our own immoral behavior. In His great love for us, He will sometimes allow us to experience the embarrassing, even shameful, consequences of our actions.

A reputation that takes a lifetime to build can be destroyed in a matter of minutes. That's why there is simply no room in the life of a Christian for compromising with the moral pollution of this world. If we rationalize immorality, we open ourselves up to guilt and shame. But if we flee immorality, as God tells us to, we will never regret it. It's a wonderful feeling to be forgiven, to know that God has removed your sin and shame from you. But there's something even better than being forgiven, and that's avoiding the sin and shame in the first place.

Politically Incorrect

I once appeared as one of the four guest panelists on ABC's late-night TV talk show *Politically Incorrect,* hosted by comedian Bill Maher. In case you've never seen the show, the format is like this: Bill Maher brings on a liberal comedian, a liberal actor, a liberal journalist, and one person who is politically or morally conservative. Then Bill Maher and the other liberals beat up on the conservative. The show always revolves around current topics or headline stories.

The night I was on, the question was, "Is it better for teens to have oral sex so they don't get pregnant, or is it better for them to have normal intercourse with condoms?" Those were the only options! The show is "live tape," meaning it's taped in full for later broadcast, but they don't stop the tape and do retakes, so it's as good as being live. If you make a mistake, you can't take it back.

One of the other panelists was a young actress in a suit and low-cut shirt that was obviously designed to advertise her cleavage. At one point, she said, "We women dress the way we do because we're trying to snag ourselves a husband. That's why we have sex with you guys—we figure if you get to sample the merchandise, maybe you'll want to buy."

One of the male panelists pounced on that. "That's why we guys are always taking advantage of you. Why should I buy the cow if I can get the milk for free? I see girls like you, dressed like you are with that exposed cleavage, and I've gotta tell you, you're just asking for trouble. You're an open invitation. You're just asking me to have sex with you."

At that point, I glanced down at my own outfit—I was glad I was dressed modestly!

"You bet!" the young woman shot back. "It *is* an invitation! We're just going to snag a husband, and we'll do it any way we can. It's absolutely true—the way we dress sends a message, and I know you guys pick up on that. The way a woman dresses is intentional. It's designed to say, 'I'm available,' or, 'I'm not available.' That's up to a woman, if she wants to put out a message like that or not." And the conversation swirled on from there.

I sat there for the first three or four minutes, listening to the opinions fly like bouncing Ping-Pong balls, not hearing a single word about morality or God or the emotional harm of teen sex or the need for self-respect or the fact that neither condoms nor oral sex offers full protection against sexually transmitted disease. And I was thinking, *Thanks a lot, Lord! I know You want me to say something here, and I know what You want me to say. I also know that as soon as I open my mouth, they'll be all over me—but here goes . . .*

So I said, "You know what? You're all talking about the wrong thing. The issue is not whether teenagers should have oral sex or use a condom. The issue we should be talking about is that *all* sex outside of marriage is a sin against God, and a sin against your physical and emotional health—whether you're a teenager or an adult."

There were two or three beats of stunned silence while my words hung in the air—then a few of the older people in the studio audience went clap-clap-clap.

Bill Maher smirked and said, "You got a smattering of applause there, Kim. I don't think that opinion went over very big."

"It's not my opinion to give," I replied. "Look, I'm too stupid to figure out what's right or wrong on my own. I have to read the Bible to know what God wants me to do—and God says that sex outside of marriage is wrong, it's harmful. Sin has consequences, and it affects more than just the person who commits the sin. God's moral law was given to us to protect us, not to hurt us. If we want to protect teenagers from pregnancy, emotional harm, and disease, we don't say, 'Here, take this condom,' or, 'Try this sexual technique or that position.' We have to say, 'Respect yourself, and wait for marriage.'"

At that point, Bill Maher really came after me. He asked me if I was a virgin when I was married. Of course, having been in a "trial marriage" before making it legal, I had to answer no. But that, of course, was before I was a born-again Christian, before I understood the moral values I now embrace. I started to answer his question, but he cut me off, laughed at me, and wouldn't let me explain.

Bill Maher was tougher on me than most interviewers usually are. People tend to go easy on me because they know I don't go out of my way to pick a fight—I just give my opinion. They know that whatever I say is nothing more or less than my heartfelt beliefs. But I got beat up a little on *Politically Incorrect*. Oh, it wasn't too bad—certainly not as bad as, say, being nailed to a cross. But I'm not in any hurry to repeat the experience.

The point I made on the show still stands, and it's the point of everything I'm saying in these pages: The world may hate God's moral rules. The world may do everything possible to get around His rules for living. The world may think God is cruel, vindictive, judgmental, and unfair. But God is right, and the world is wrong. God is love, and the world is polluted with sin. God's rules were given not to wreck our fun but to guard us from harm, to enrich our sexual experiences, and to give our lives meaning.

The world says it's impossible to live a pure life. But you and

I know better. It's not only possible to live a pure life in a polluted world, it is absolutely essential. It's the only way to live.

There's a price to pay for speaking out for faith and morality in the world today. The ones who pollute the world with immorality get all the applause and attention. Those who talk about purity and morality get laughed at and booed off the stage. So it takes courage to make a stand for what's right—but we're not afraid of a little ridicule, are we?

Okay, we know what we have to do. First, we have to purify ourselves within. Once we've done that, we're ready to take on the world!

6

Building Whole
Families in a
Broken World

My children have put up with a lot from their divorced parents. I have one set of ideas about parenting, family rules, discipline, nutrition, health care, spirituality, and so forth. My ex-husband, James, and Bobby's father, has another set of ideas. He and I try to work together on these issues, but there are strong differences between many of his convictions and mine. Resolving these differences is made all the more complex by the fact that my ex-husband and I live at opposite ends of the country.

It brings tears to my eyes to see how our grown-up problems sometimes invade the lives of our children. For example, James, my oldest, has a medical problem that causes his thyroid gland not to manufacture enough thyroid hormone (it's genetic—I have the same problem). It's a condition that is easily managed with thyroid hormone replacement therapy. This therapy doesn't involve drugs or chemicals—just a natural hormone that everyone needs, and that James's body doesn't adequately produce. But when James went to his father's house, his dad wouldn't allow him to take the thyroid hormone because he believed I had our son on some powerful drug (he has since reluctantly agreed to allow James to take his medication).

Now, my ex-husband and I are both committed to eating healthy foods and drinking pure water—but on the issue of this thyroid hormone therapy, he and I have disagreed. James's father loves him very much and truly wants the best for him, as do I. We both feel we would be doing James a disservice if we did anything other than what we are doing—and poor James is caught in the middle. When James is in my house, he lives under one set of conditions and rules, and when he visits his father, he lives under another.

So James and his brother Bobby live in a broken world. Their world split apart when their mother and father separated and divorced. There's no going back to the way things were before the divorce. All of us, including James and Bobby, have to deal with life *as it is now.* Somehow, Ron and I, working in cooperation with my ex-husband, have to find a way to raise whole, healthy kids, and to build a whole, healthy family in this broken world.

The boys have asked me if Ron and I will stay together. It hurts to know that they have this worry in mind. It hurts to think that perhaps they don't fully trust marriage because my first marriage ended in divorce. But I was glad they felt they could ask me about it, because it gave us a chance to talk. I have been able to completely assure them that, with God, prayer, and the Bible in the center of our life together, Ron and I will stay together through thick and thin, fulfilling the marriage covenant we made to each other before God.

So if you are thinking about divorce, don't read this and think, *Well, Kim did it and everything turned out okay for her.*

No, it didn't. It was unbelievably painful. I was hurt, my husband was hurt, my kids were hurt. Of course, there are extreme situations where divorce is better than staying together—the so-called "Three A's," abuse, adultery, and addiction. But, in general, I tell others who are working on a difficult marriage, "Keep working at it! Don't think that divorce is an easy way out of a painful situation. The pain you have now is not as bad as the pain of divorce!"

I have to be candid about this: Being divorced and remarried really does make me feel intimidated when I go out and talk about family values and morality. I'm not proud of my divorce; I'm embarrassed by it. I separated and went back to my ex-husband twice before it finally became clear there was no choice but divorce. It was not something I wanted. It simply *is*.

But the pain of divorce enables me to speak with authenticity about divorce—and about the importance of healthy, intact families. Having felt the pain of divorce, and having seen its effect on my kids, I have become passionate, even fanatical, about keeping my present marriage strong, and about defending marriage in our society. And in the process and aftermath of my own divorce, I've learned a lot about what it takes to keep a marriage healthy and whole.

Ron and I have what is commonly called a "blended family." He brings two daughters from a previous marriage, I bring two sons from a previous marriage, and we have made one son, Noah, together. I can truly say that we are one big happy family, because we have wrapped our family around a common center—that is, around Jesus Christ. Do we have our problems and hassles? Oh, lots! We have adjustments and scheduling conflicts and the usual sibling stuff—but we are happy, we are healthy, we are making it work.

Ron had a family that was broken and so did I. We put our

broken families together and made a whole one. Not a perfect family, but a family that functions well, faces problems honestly, and hangs together with love, understanding, acceptance, and forgiveness.

With all the pressures and temptations that confront us in today's world, it's not easy to build whole and healthy families—but it can be done. I know, because Ron and I are doing it. We make our share of mistakes, but we are committed to seeing ourselves and our kids through for life, and by God's grace, we're getting the job done. Here are some of the things I've learned about building whole families in a broken world:

1. Everything starts with prayer.

My husband and I often pray together. I frequently tell him, "Ron, I don't pray as well without you. You're my other half." Sometimes, if I feel a need to talk to God, I go find Ron. He will drop whatever he's doing, get down on his knees with me, and we'll join our hearts together in prayer.

We pray together most nights before bed. Ron is more of a night owl than I am, so sometimes I have to go downstairs and find him. I just feel something's not right without him, and that I'm much better with him. So I find Ron and say, "Hey! I'm going to bed, and I need you to pray with me!" And he does.

The Bible talks about the mystical union between a husband and a wife: "They are no longer two, but one."[1] Many people think that this verse refers only to the sexual, emotional, or relational union between husband and wife, but I believe it refers to two people who become one in a spiritual sense, united in prayer, fused together in their relationship with God.

Sometimes I'll be praying alone beside my bed, and Ron will

come into the room and begin to talk to me—then he'll see me on my knees and say, "Sorry, didn't mean to bother you."

Bother me! "Come here!" I call out. "You make it better!" And he gets down on his knees beside me, and we come into God's presence together. It's so much more complete when it's the two of us. As Jesus said, "For where two or three are gathered together in My name, I am there in the midst of them."[2]

Ron and I want our children to see that prayer is a natural, daily, spontaneous part of our lives. We pray with our kids at just any old time—before going to the circus or a movie or before school. We stop and pray for a need, or we just pause and thank God for the sunshine or the rain or for friends who come over to play. When we hear an ambulance go by with the siren blaring, I call the kids together and we ask God to help and protect the patient in the ambulance.

We also pray with the children during the difficult times. There are times when the boys get rowdy or they argue or they are just a little too loud and active, and I'm over the limit of what I can tolerate. Sometimes I just let it all out in a big yell— not because I think that's a good way to parent, but because I just can't contain it anymore. And you know what? It gets their attention! And I say something like, "Look at what I just did! I yelled at you—and I don't want to yell at you! And God doesn't want me to yell at you, either. You're my children and I love you, but when you behave like this, I don't want to be around you!"

"Why not, Mommy?" they ask, wide-eyed.

"Because you're not listening, you're not obeying, you're not being nice to one another or to me. Do you think God is pleased when you behave like this—or do you think it makes Him sad?"

"Sad," they say, hanging their heads.

"Well, I have an idea—let's make God happy! Let's talk to Him and tell Him how sorry we are. I'm going to tell Him I'm sorry for yelling, and you're going to tell Him you're sorry for not obeying and for making Him sad. And then we'll ask Him to help us obey."

So I ask one of the boys to pray, or I lead in prayer, we talk to God, then we go about our business with a vastly improved attitude—myself included!

I believe that in order to have a healthy home, you must have a peaceful home. When there is arguing, when family members are not happy with one another, I think that often signals that it is a good time to pray. We may not *feel* like praying at such times, but that's when we need prayer the most! Fact is, I sometimes start praying through clenched teeth! But before long, I'm happy that we stopped and took the time to reconnect with God. When we keep the lines of communication open with God, He helps us to keep the lines of communication open with each other.

This is not to say that a healthy home never experiences problems, stress, tension, or conflict. Rather, a healthy family has learned how to bring peace out of stressful situations, and how to resolve conflict in a healthy way. And peace begins with prayer.

Philippians 4:6–7 tells us, "Be anxious for nothing, but in everything by prayer and supplication, with thanksgiving, let your requests be made known to God; and the peace of God, which surpasses all understanding, will guard your hearts and minds through Christ Jesus" (NKJV). That's where the peace of God is found: in prayer, supplication, thanksgiving, and making our requests known to God. This is as true in our family life as it is in our individual lives.

Our children attend Christian schools. Recently, awards

were given to the various children in James's fifth-grade class—awards for academic achievement, athletic achievement, and so forth. James was given the award for "Most Spiritual Student" in the class. He really does have a heart for Jesus Christ, and he loves to bring new children to Sunday school. One day his teacher told me he had gotten up and given his testimony before the class, and a dozen of his classmates responded by making a commitment to Jesus Christ that day.

When James won the "Most Spiritual" award at school, however, he was disappointed. He likes to be thought of as a good athlete, and he really wanted one of the sports awards. He came home a little downcast and told me, "Gee, Mom, I thought I'd be best at this or that—but all I got was 'Most Spiritual.'"

"Jamie," I said, "that's the best award there is! What's more important in this world than having a relationship with Jesus? Good grades and excelling at sports or music are terrific—but if you could only win one prize in life, the one you should want is 'Most Spiritual.'"

He smiled and said, "Yeah, I guess you're right." And he was fine with it after that.

It's exciting to see him grow and mature as a Christian young man. One Sunday, not long ago, our family was in church. At one point during the sermon I leaned over to whisper something to James, and he whispered back, "Shh! I'm trying to listen to the sermon!" I have never been so glad to be rebuked as I was right then and there. It's a thrill to see that James is developing a mature interest in spiritual things. That's the kind of maturity I'm working, day by day, to build into my own life and the lives of my kids—and it all begins with prayer.

2. Keep the communication lines open.

My husband and I don't fight. I know what you're thinking: *Every* married couple fights. That's what I used to think too. But Ron and I don't—and I have to give Ron the credit for that. We talk, we even argue in a calm, controlled fashion, but we have never had an occasion of yelling at each other, insulting or name-calling, bickering, anger, or rage. We never sat down and set out rules. It just seems that we have a natural way of communicating so that we discuss everything without fighting.

I think one of the reasons we relate to each other so well and communicate with each other so openly is that we have both been through divorce, and we are 100 percent focused on making this marriage a success. I know what bothered and hurt Ron in his first marriage, and I consciously steer away from those kinds of behaviors and toward the kinds of actions that promote peace, understanding, and harmony in our relationship.

We both take the Bible seriously when it says not to let the sun go down on anger. Fact is, I have to take that scriptural command more to heart than Ron does, because he's very easy-going and never really gets angry. I know that in the past I have been more prone to be argumentative and to pick fights when I'm feeling tired, irritable, and sensitive. I still get that way—but Ron never feels threatened, even when I'm in a cranky mood. Sometimes I come to him and say, "I'm bothered about something. We need to talk."

"We don't have a problem," he says. "You're a little tired. Just go to bed. You'll feel better in the morning."

"No," I say, "this is really bothering me now. I feel really icky inside. I know it's just me, but I've got to work this out with you." And I sit down in front of him and make him talk about it. He can see I'm not going to go to bed, so he puts down his newspaper or clicks off the TV and he gives me his full attention.

After I've laid everything out, he says, "I love you. Now go to bed." It just takes a few minutes, we work it out, and I'm fine. We never hold grudges, and we never go to bed angry. We work it out.

If there is any problem between us, Ron and I say, "*This* is the problem we have to solve together, and I want to work with you to solve it." We don't say, "*You* are the problem." When there is conflict, we see each other as partners and players on the same team—not as opponents.

Again, prayer is an essential part of the way we relate to each other. Once I talk to God about a problem, I hear Him saying to me, "Kim, Ron's wrong about this, but you're wrong about that. Take responsibility!" God gives me a little kick in the caboose, and that's when I need to go to Ron and say, "God has shown me that I was wrong about this and this, but I was hurt or annoyed when you did this, that, and the other thing." And Ron's always very open to hear my concerns. He usually doesn't say much, but he listens, and he changes things for the better. If a wife can say, "I was wrong about this," the husband doesn't need to be so defensive, and he can admit that he was wrong too.

One of the problems in many marriages, I believe, is that we women tend to treat communication as a game of manipulation. Women love to play that game: "If you really loved me, I wouldn't have to tell you what I feel and what I want." Men hate that. Men are very direct, and they respect and appreciate it when we level with them, straight up. When wives screech, scream, or scheme, men avoid or retreat or just plain shut down! But if we just say, candidly and honestly, "This is what's going on, this is how I feel, this is what I need," a man will usually say, "That's cool, I can deal with that."

I've learned that blaming is a relationship-killer. It's important, in any conflict or problem, to take blame off the table. Husbands and wives could solve their problems a lot more quickly if they stopped focusing on assigning fault and instead focused on solving the problem. Example:

SHE: "When you contradicted me in front of the children, I felt my authority with them was undermined."

HE: "That's not it. I didn't intend to undermine you, I was only trying to suggest another way of looking at the situation."

SHE: "I know you didn't intend to undermine me, but that's the way I felt. I'm not saying you did it to hurt me, I'm saying you had good intentions, but I was hurt by the way you handled it. I'm not saying that what you said was wrong—just that it was not good to contradict me in front of the kids. So, because I know you love me, I'm asking you to not do this again. Next time, take me aside privately, where the children can't hear—just like I'm doing with you now—so that I won't feel undermined in front of them."

HE: "Okay, that makes sense."

What's true of marital communication is also true of parent-to-child and child-to-child communication. Ron and I try to keep the communication lines open among all members of the family. There are times when the children just drive me up the wall with their noise or bickering, and I will say—with my anger and frustration clearly on display!—"All right, kids! That's it! I've had it! Let's pray!" (Not exactly a gracious call to worship, but hey, this is an emergency!)

Sometimes my kids will respond, "I don't want to pray with

you!" They know that prayer will heal the relationship—and they don't want that! They want to hang on to the anger! That's only natural and human—and both children and adults often feel that way. But I put my foot down. I have a responsibility as a Christian parent to make sure we come together as a family and solve the problem together—not as opponents but as members of the same team.

Problem solving and conflict resolution can be tricky when you are dealing with young children. As I write this, James is twelve years old, Bobby is nine, and Noah is four. James is mature enough that he enjoys being Noah's big brother. But Bobby is just at that age when he often finds his little brother to be more of an annoyance than a buddy. So there's a lot of conflict between Bobby and Noah. That's normal, of course, because of their ages.

Bobby will say to Noah, "I'll race you!" And, of course, Bobby beats little Noah by a mile, and he says, "I won! I beat you!" So I say, "Well, honey, of course you did. You're five years older than Noah. Instead of trying to beat him, why don't you just play with him or watch a movie with him?"

Or Bobby will come in and say, "Mommy, Noah just called me an idiot!" And I say, "Where do you think he learned that word? Listen, Bobby, you're Noah's big brother, and he loves you and looks up to you. You're teaching him by the way you behave toward him. All these big-boy things you do, he's going to copy. Why don't you try letting him win? Why don't you try playing with him on his level?" Well, Bobby's not quite old enough to get this concept, so he and Noah keep butting heads.

But James, being older, doesn't see himself as being in competition with Noah, so he'll go up to his brother and say, "Hit me right here in the shoulder." And Noah will give him a little four-year-old child's jab, and James will fall down and make a big production out of it. "Oh! That hurts! You hit too hard, Noah! You don't know your own strength!" And little Noah gets the biggest kick out of it.

James does little-boy things with Noah because he knows that's what Noah enjoys. "Let's watch this cartoon, Noah," he says. "It's the best!" Or, "You make the best sand castles, Noah!" Or, "Let's ride your little scooter, Noah!" James just thinks Noah is the best little guy. When James races Noah, Noah wins! And that makes Noah laugh—"I beat that big guy!"—and when Noah laughs, James is happy.

I'd like Bobby to be able to play with Noah the way James does, but that's just not going to happen until Bobby gets older and more mature. Ron and I have to deal with each of our kids at his or her own level, but our goal is that each of our children learns to deal with anger and conflict in a healthy, understanding, spiritually mature way. We try to teach principles of healthy communication to our kids—and we try to model those principles in our daily lives.

3. Take personal responsibility.

Ron and I recognize that we both must take 100 percent responsibility for our relationship. Some people say that marriage is a fifty-fifty proposition, but that's wrong. When you try to divide a marriage right down the middle and say, "These are my responsibilities and these are your responsibilities," you have a prescription for trouble. After all, what do you call it when you divide a marriage in half? Divorce! Marriage is a union, it's about becoming one.

In order for two to become one, both partners must take complete responsibility for the entire marriage. That means you stop bickering over who's not pulling 50 percent of the load or who is trespassing on the other person's 50 percent of the turf. Only when both sides accept 100 percent of the responsibility for the relationship can the marriage really function as God intended it to.

So Ron and I try to model personal responsibility, and we try to teach it to our children. For example, James was feeling very frustrated with his schoolwork—and he was blaming his teacher. "My teacher's mean," he said. "She picks on me and gives me bad grades." Well, I want to stick up for my son as much as the next parent, but the fact is that James has a learning disability called attention deficit hyperactive disorder (ADHD). He's a wonderful kid, but he has a shorter attention span in class and he doesn't get very good grades.

So I said to him, "Jamie, your teacher isn't mean. You have a problem, but you're working on it. I'll stick with you and we'll work it out together, okay?"

"But I don't understand!" he complained. "This isn't fair! Other kids don't have this problem. Why am I going through this?"

"Everybody's unique, everyone has special abilities and special problems. There are some things you do better than other kids, and there are some things you don't do as well. You're *you,* and that's a wonderful thing to be. So don't worry about anything. God has a wonderful future planned for you—a future that is as special and unique as you are."

After that little talk, I never heard James blame his teacher again. We worked together on his schoolwork so that he wouldn't fall behind, and he's doing fine. Taking personal responsibility can be a tough concept for kids—and for adults—but we can never become truly whole and healthy until we accept ourselves and accept responsibility for who we are and what we do.

4. Build memories and traditions together.

Memories and traditions are the glue that holds a family together over time. They build within each family member a sense of security, a sense that there are rhythms, customs, and observances in the life of the family that can be counted on, day by day, year by year. It is good for our children to know that we join our hearts in prayer at mealtimes and every night before bedtime.

In our family, we make a point of making and storing memories—from family vacations in Florida (you should see us riding in the golf cart, singing together!) to playing hockey games in the driveway to simply spending weekends at home, doing yardwork while our sheep and goats run around in the backyard. The boys love to shoot baskets and play H.O.R.S.E. with Ron—even though he always wins. What matters is the time spent (and memories collected) as we are together as a family.

It's important to have certain traditions that can always be counted on at Easter, Thanksgiving, and Christmas. It's also important to remember what these traditions are about: faith, family, and love. A lot of people are sticklers about celebrating a certain calendar date and forget to celebrate and practice what that calendar date is supposed to mean. For example, some couples spend a lot of time battling each other over whose family they are going to be with on December 25—and in the process, they completely forget about what Christmas is supposed to *mean:* the birth of the Savior, the love and forgiveness of God the Father, and demonstrating that same quality of love to family and friends in the form of thoughtful gifts.

One way we can demonstrate the true meaning of Christmas is by giving a sacrificial gift to our mate and our mate's family: "Let's spend Christmas Day with your family this year, and we can spend Christmas Eve or New Year's Day or some other day with my family. It's not the calendar date that matters, but the true meaning of the season that is really important."

Ron and I, because of the careers we have, live very mobile lives. Sometimes we are called to work on Thanksgiving Day or other holidays, and sometimes the call doesn't come until the last minute. So we've learned to take things as they come, and to be flexible about dates and seasons and traditions.

One time, when my parents were visiting us from New York state, I got a call from Larry King, asking me to guest-host his TV talk show on CNN while he was out of town. It happened that the date he gave me was my anniversary. I checked with Ron, and he said, "Fine. Do the show."

But when I told my parents, they were horrified! "You can't do that!" they said. "It's your anniversary! You need to go out and have dinner and give each other presents and cards!"

I just smiled and said, "No, we don't. We'll be just as much in love with each other the following day, so we'll celebrate then." The way I see it, you don't get a chance to host *Larry King Live* every day. If I'm okay with it and Ron's okay with it, then I'll do the show and we'll celebrate later.

As it turned out, Larry's flight to Dallas was canceled, so he stayed in L.A. and hosted the show himself. Too bad—I had my Larry King suspenders all ready for the show. At least I got to go on his show as a guest that night, and it was a lot of fun. The point is that while it is important to maintain family traditions and observances, we must also be flexible, focusing more on family, faith, and the true meaning of the season—not just on a particular date on a calendar.

5. Give children the structure and boundaries they want and need.

Children really want rules. They feel more secure playing in a fenced-in yard than in a wide-open field beside a freeway.

Boundaries provide safety and dependability. Even though children may rebel at times against this rule or that restriction, overall a child finds the structure of routines, rules, and limits to be reassuring and comforting. When a child tests those boundaries, it is not so much because he wants to break the rules as to simply make sure they're still there, providing security and protection.

The Bible tells us that our yes should mean yes, and our no should mean no. In other words, as parents, we need to follow through when we say yes or no. I have one child who is a born negotiator—he always tests my yes and my no! I've learned that the more my children test my yes and no, the more I need to make sure I stand firm.

In the Duguay family, for example, we have rules about nutrition. We have water filters on all the drinking taps in the house, and we drink pure water at mealtimes. Sometimes, other children from school or the neighborhood will come to our house to play and have lunch, and they'll come to the table at lunchtime and say, "Can I have soda to drink?"

"No," I say. "But you can have a glass of water."

"But I want a soda! I have soda all the time at home!"

"At my house," I reply, "when you're thirsty, you have water."

And they drink their water and find out that they not only survive it—it tastes good!

Sometimes I'll be out somewhere with my kids and their friends, and the kids will ask me to buy them snacks from a vending machine. My kids know not to expect me to buy them candy bars, and they are happy just to have anything from a vending machine—for some reason, food that comes out of a vending machine is more fun to eat than food that comes out of a refrigerator. But the other kids will often beg, "Please buy us candy!" I reply, "My money doesn't buy candy.

It only buys healthy snacks like fruit or bagel chips or pretzels." They may beg a few more times, but pretty soon they see that I will not budge—and they settle for the healthy snacks.

The point is, we have rules. They are house rules, family rules, and they apply to everyone, even guests. And that enables my own kids to have a dependable, reliable structure in their lives. They know that, even when company comes to play and share our table, or when they go with us to the amusement park or someplace else, we don't abandon our rules. We don't wash down our good food with fizzy, sugar-laden, caffeine-laced junk-drinks or buy sugary, fatty candy bars from vending machines.

There is a saying that rules are made to be broken. I say rules are made to keep us and our families whole and healthy. Our job as parents is to make sure that our children have the protective structure to enable them to grow up behaving responsibly and feeling secure.

6. Transmit healthy, family-centered values to the next generation.

Children of divorce are statistically more likely to become divorced as adults, or to reject marriage altogether in favor of simply living together. I want to spare my children the pain of divorce, and I want them to honor and value the covenant of marriage. I pray often that each of my boys will make a wise choice of a wife and that each will have a healthy Christian marriage. I also tell them that I am praying for these specific blessings in their future lives.

Having gone through the pain of divorce ourselves, my husband and I know the importance of teaching our children the importance of making a wise mate selection, of making commitments and keeping covenants, and of building an intact, healthy family. Ron and I are committed to transmitting healthy, family-centered values to our kids.

In teaching our kids about morality and values, we need to go beyond merely trying to scare them about the risk of AIDS and other diseases. We need to inspire them with a positive reason for keeping themselves pure. I didn't hear very much about biblical, moral purity when I was growing up—and I wish I had. We need to help our kids see their lives as dedicated and consecrated to God, their bodies as temples of the Holy Spirit, and their sexuality and emotional makeup as holy gifts from God, to be used with honor. We need to help our children to understand that sex is an act that unites two into one, and if there is no protective covenant of marriage surrounding that sexual union, both people lose a part of themselves.

Girls used to be brought up to respect themselves, and to cherish and defend their virginity. Today, we no longer tell girls to be good—we just tell them to be careful. And that's why many girls are selling themselves short. Girls today are so happy to have some greasy, tattoo-spattered guy want them, they don't look beyond the next twenty minutes to see what kind of a future they are going to have. Too often, a girl fails to stop and realize that once this boy gets what he wants, she is going to be alone again—alone with a baby or a disease, alone with years of guilt and pain.

We also need to teach our children that there is a lot more to a good marriage than romantic attraction. So-called "love"—feeling emotionally drawn to another person—is not a sufficient basis for marriage. There must be several key ingredients, all working together, in order for a marriage to be healthy and enduring.

First, there must be a common bond of faith. That is what the Bible means when it says that Christians should not be "unequally yoked" with non-Christians. It makes no sense for a Christian to marry a non-Christian, because together they cannot share the most important aspect of life—a relationship with Jesus Christ. If they don't have their faith in common, there are so many other things they won't have in common—common values and morality, a common framework of biblical rules for solving problems and settling disagreements, a common sense of accountability to Christian leadership and the Christian community, and a common sense of what vows and covenants mean. That is why, before Ron and I got married, I made sure that he had been born again.

Second, people who are contemplating marriage must have significant goals, ideals, and values in sync. That doesn't mean that these two people must be as identical as clones. It is healthy, in fact, if there are areas where their personalities differ and complement each other. I'm grateful that my husband, Ron, brings to our marriage so many qualities and traits that I lack. Together, we are more complete.

Third, there must be genuine Christlike love. In his book *Questions Couples Ask Behind Closed Doors,* psychologist and marriage counselor James Osterhaus explains what this love is all about:

> The ancient Greeks and Hebrews—in whose languages the Bible was originally written—appear to have been wiser in matters of love than we are. They had many words for love, and each word had a specific connotation. The Hebrews used the word *hesed* to denote "covenant love," love which is rooted in loyalty and faithfulness to a promise or covenant. This form of love is expressed in commitment.
>
> The Greeks had a parallel word for the Hebrew concept of *hesed.* Their word was *agape.* Although you find this

word used only a very few times in classical Greek literature, it is lavished profusely throughout the Greek New
Testament. *Agape*-love seeks the good of another person
not because of emotional attachment, not because that person has earned the right to be loved, but simply because a
prior commitment (a promise) has been made. *Agape*-love
does not derive from the fact that the other person is lov-
able or valuable. Rather, it actually *creates* value in the person being loved.[3]

So it's crucial that a husband and wife have more in common than mere sexual magnetism or romantic emotions. Feelings come and go, but faith, goals, values, covenants, and
Christlike *agape* love endure, and will carry a couple through
the dry spells and rough spots of life.

As my son James turned twelve, I could see that he was
growing in his awareness of the opposite sex and their awareness of him. He's a very handsome young man, and the girls
really flock around him. James is at that stage where he thinks
it's cool to have a girlfriend—but he's not sure what he's supposed to do with girls. Do you hold hands or not? What do
you talk to girls about? He's a few years away from actually
dating girls—but he is becoming more intrigued by girls all
the time.

I've had talks with James about the opposite sex, about
God's will for his moral purity, about the fact that he needs to
respect himself and others. I've even talked with him about the
kind of woman he should want to marry someday. There's an
old Roy Orbison song I like that says:

> Some people say she's not pretty; they don't realize
> That beauty's often hidden from another's eyes

James and I were talking about that song, and I told him, "Remember, a woman like that who truly loves Jesus and who truly loves you will be a much better wife than a beauty queen whose heart is all wrong. Don't get focused on the outward appearance, but on the person inside. You know, I pray for you that you will find a wonderful Christian girl who loves you and who loves Jesus even more."

I know that the kind of wife I am to Ron will have a big effect on James's idea of what to look for in a wife. It's not enough just to talk about the kind of woman James should look for—I also have to *be* that kind of woman. I have to exemplify a vibrant, vital relationship with Jesus Christ.

Do I make mistakes? You bet! But Ron is very quick to get me back on track. Here's an example: You've probably seen parents who push their kids' interest in the opposite sex. They say, "Oh, wouldn't it be cute for little Johnny to have a little girlfriend? Johnny, don't you want to call your girlfriend on the phone? Did you give her a valentine?" You guessed it—I was starting to do this kind of stuff with James. Ron took me aside and said, "Don't do that. Don't try to get Jamie interested in girls—he's too young for that. Just wait till he's ready—that day will come soon enough."

Ron was right. He admonished me, and I stopped doing it. Kids start dating and getting romantic notions way too young as it is—and we parents shouldn't be trying to start them any younger, no matter how "cute" we think it is. Preadolescence is a time of growth and exploration for children. It's a golden time in which we, as parents, are to instill in them a sense of values, a sense of right and wrong, a belief system, a strong sense of family.

After all, what is the most decisive factor in determining a child's future? Is it the economic status of his parents? The color of his skin? His or her gender? Genes? Background? Education? Toilet training? No. I really believe the one factor that, more than anything else, decides a child's future is that child's *values*.

A child's first, most influential, and most indispensable teachers are his parents. Children are a gift from the Lord, a sacred responsibility placed in our hands by a loving heavenly Father. We have a duty before God to use every available moment as an opportunity to teach our children about Jesus, about moral behavior, about respect for self and others, about integrity and truthfulness, about honor, about making wise choices, and about the importance of family.

What Are "Family Values"?

During the last couple of elections, there was a lot of talk about something called "family values," but rarely did you hear the politicians take time to define what is meant by that term. To me, "family values" is a pretty simple idea. It doesn't need to be redefined or reevaluated. The family is the most fundamental unit of society, and it consists of people who are related by marriage, by "blood" or close genetic kinship, or by adoption. The ideal family situation is a loving mother, a loving father, and the children they make together or adopt—and they all stay together and live happily ever after. Obviously, many parents do not fully achieve that ideal. I didn't achieve it, but it was certainly my goal and my ideal.

It's still my goal to raise James and Bobby in such a way that they always have a loving mom and a loving stepdad, and that they see their bio-dad at every opportunity. It's still my goal to make sure that Noah never has to go through the disruption of divorce that his older brothers went through. I intend to make sure that none of my kids is ever deprived of the stability, security, permanence, and values of an intact, two-parent, Christian family.

Are there other arrangements of family besides the traditional mom-dad-kids arrangement? Certainly. The boys and I were a family when we lived in our little apartment in New York. We were not an *ideal* family. We were a *struggling* family. Our circumstances were considerably less than perfect. It was a difficult time for all of us. But we were a family.

The fact is, the farther we get from the traditional ideal of family, the more difficult life is for everyone concerned, especially the children. I have a lot of respect for single mothers who get up every day and face the difficult task of earning a living while raising good kids. We should never condemn the single mother who struggles to raise her kids under such difficult conditions—but at the same time, we shouldn't offer incentives for women to become single mothers.

For years, our government has paid welfare benefits to single mothers, cut off those benefits if mom got married, and penalized marriage through the tax code. After watching the destruction of countless families, we are finally waking up to the fact that the best antipoverty program of all is not welfare—it's a strong family. The biggest poverty problem we have in America today is a poverty of family values. Children don't need a government program as much as they need a mom and a dad.

"Family values" means nothing more nor less than that we *value family:* fathers, mothers, sisters, brothers, grandparents, aunts and uncles, cousins, and yes, stepfathers and stepmothers in many cases. We must also value adoptive parents and adoptive kids—there are so many kids who live in institutions or foster care who need the security and permanence of a two-parent family.

Some people will argue that talking about "family values" is just a sneaky attack on nontraditional living arrangements, such as gay unions, "shack-up" couples, and single parents. No, lifting up the family and upholding family values does not mean putting down those who are not in traditional families. We live in a free country, and people can pretty much choose any lifestyle or living arrangement they wish. Gays are free to form relationships and unions on any terms they wish, and unmarried couples are free to "shack up" if they so choose.

But marriage deserves special protection. Those who talk about "spousal equivalents" and "significant others," and who want to make gay unions and cohabiting the equivalent of marriage are really trivializing marriage and endangering the future of our children. Our society can only endure as long as we uphold marriage and family as the ideal.

The family provides a growing, nurturing, blessing, healthy environment for raising the next generation. Whatever criticism and hostility may come our way from the "anything-goes" fringe of our society, we have to boldly tell the world that not all living arrangements are created equal. There is a right way and a wrong way to raise kids, and the wrong way is to deprive kids of an intact family and to hand over parental responsibility to the government or the "village" or any other institutional caretaker. As someone once said, the family is the first and best "department of health, education, and welfare."

Our nation was built on the foundation of healthy families, and it will be healthy families that rebuild America and make it a strong, healthy nation once more. There is a story in the Old Testament book of Nehemiah that has a lot to say to us about how we should protect and preserve our families and our society. Many years before Christ, the city of Jerusalem was destroyed by foreign armies. When the prophet Nehemiah returned to the ruined city, he found that the city walls were leveled and the city itself was overrun by criminals. The people of the city lived in constant terror.

Nehemiah's solution was to begin with the family. He gave each family a section of the city wall and told them to rebuild that section. When enemies threatened the rebuilding of the wall, Nehemiah said to the people, "Do not be afraid of them. Remember the Lord, great and awesome, and fight for your brethren, your sons, your daughters, your wives, and your houses."⁴ In other words, the prophet Nehemiah called the people to defend their families, and the institution of the family. Following God's plan for the family, drawing upon the strength of the family, Nehemiah and the people of Jerusalem rebuilt their walls, their city, and their society. They created a strong, moral, godly nation.

And that is what we must do in America today.

How to Build a Whole, Healthy Marriage in a Broken World

Okay, I know I'm no marriage expert. But after my divorce, I did a lot of reflecting, reading, and observing, because if there was one thing I knew for sure, it was that I didn't want to go through *that* again! What's more, I believe that if we really love our kids, then the best thing Ron and I can do for them is to make our marriage as strong and healthy as it can possibly be. So here are the results of all I've learned from experience and study of what makes a marriage healthy:

1. Never yell at each other—except in case of fire, mud slide, or earthquake (that's a California rule).

2. Never let the sun go down on your anger.

3. If you have to argue or discuss an issue, stay in the present. Never dredge up old issues, old hurts, or old accusations.

4. In times of conflict, focus on behaving in a Christlike manner; focus on unconditionally loving your mate and seeking his or her benefit.

5. Never let a day go by without saying one (and preferably five or ten) affectionate, encouraging, or complimentary thing to each other.

6. Never criticize, unless it is truly intended in love and surrounded by affirmation.

7. When you argue or discuss any issue, make sure you spend *at least* 50 percent of the time listening—*really* listening, not just planning your snappy comeback. Make eye contact, nod, and repeat back what your mate said so that you know and he or she knows you really understand.

8. When you are wrong, ask for forgiveness. (And it even helps at times to ask forgiveness when you're not wrong!)

9. Never assume you can get more out of a marriage than you put in. It just won't work.

10. Never make sexual and romantic fulfillment your goal in marriage. After all, how much time do you spend in bed with your mate? And how much time do you spend relating to your mate, cooperating with your mate, interacting with your mate? Focus on loving each other and meeting each other's emotional and spiritual needs, and the sexual fulfillment will flow from the joy you bring each other throughout the day.

My marriage to Ron is precious and needs to be maintained. I have no desire to be unfaithful to him, because that would destroy the most beautiful relationship I have ever known. My faithfulness to him shields me from pain and emotional suffering. The basis of my happiness and satisfaction in life is my marriage, which is centered around our relationship with Jesus Christ. By working to make my marriage the best it can be, I find a joy that overflows into all my other relationships, especially my relationship with my children.

I thank God every day for Ron—a man who exemplifies the qualities described in Galatians 5:22–23—kindness, goodness, gentleness, self-control, and faithfulness. He also has a real love for children and looks for the truth in every situation. Ron and I have both come out of brokenness to create wholeness and a healthy relationship, centered around Jesus Christ.

All of us, no matter how "together" we may seem on the outside, have areas of brokenness in our lives. All of us live in a very broken, wounded world. But we can build whole, healthy marriages and whole, healthy families—and as we do, we bring a little bit of healing to this broken world.

7
Raising Safe, Strong Kids in a Dangerous World

You may have seen the 1998 HBO movie, *Gia, the Tragic True Story of Supermodel Gia Carangi*. Gia and I crossed paths at a number of different shoots for various magazines. I once went on a ten-day trip with her for American *Vogue*. The shoot was in the Caribbean, on St. Bart's.

Gia and I flew together from New York and shared a hotel room on the island. Right after we arrived at the hotel, I noticed that she was riffling through her bags, looking disgusted and upset. "What's wrong?" I asked.

"I lost my heroin at JFK!" she moaned.

I was about twenty-one at the time, and I was shocked. "Why do you take heroin?" I asked.

"Because it makes me feel good," she said with an edge of annoyance, as if I had just asked the lamest question in the world.

Over the next few days, I saw just how "good" she felt without her bag of heroin. She went through some very hard days where she really missed her fix. She was completely miserable while going through withdrawal. I could see she was destroying herself, but I didn't have any idea what I could do to help her.

Gia was born in Philadelphia, the youngest of three children. When she was eleven, her mother walked out of the marriage, leaving Gia at home with her dad and two brothers. Being abandoned by her mother nearly destroyed her. Like a lot of people who have been deeply, emotionally wounded, Gia tried to fill the holes in her heart with glamour, excitement, fame, and money. In 1977 she went to New York, determined to become a model, and she was soon signed by one of the biggest agents in the world, Wilhelmina.

Her career soared, taking her around the world on assignments for *Cosmo* and *Vogue,* and doing major fashion ads for Gianni Versace. When she wasn't working, Gia partied her brains out, dancing all night at Studio 54, swallowing pills and snorting cocaine to keep up her energy. She later turned to heroin and began showing up for assignments with needle tracks in her arms, too loaded to function. Modeling jobs began to dry up, and she descended to the depths of depravity to get money for drugs. Despite several efforts to get into rehab and break free of her habit, Gia remained hooked to the end. In late 1985, she was diagnosed with advanced AIDS—probably from an infected needle.

Sometime in 1986 she decided to kill herself—but she wanted to die high. So she went out on the street to buy enough heroin to do herself in. Instead of scoring heroin, she was assaulted and severely beaten by a gang of street addicts. On November 18, 1986, at age twenty-six, Gia Carangi died of complications due to AIDS.

Gia had been to the top of the world—and she descended as far as any human being can go. What a terrible waste of beauty, talent, and life!

A Place Called Home

It's a dangerous world out there—and our job as parents is to prepare our children to handle its pressures, perils, and temptations. We must strengthen and "bulletproof" our kids against these dangers—and give them a place to come home to when the pressures become too great. At age eighteen, I emerged from the warm cocoon of my family and entered the moral battle zones of New York City, Rome, and Paris. I always knew I had a refuge waiting for me, a warm and welcoming house in upstate New York I could run to and hide in. That place of refuge is called a *family*.

I was so lucky to have had that refuge in my life. Gia didn't— and that may be what truly destroyed her.

A modeling career is not like a regular job. It pays a lot of money, but it also demands a lot from you. What most people don't realize is that the modeling world is terribly hard on your self-esteem. Sure, while the cameras are clicking, it's, "Darling, you're wonderful! Beautiful! Perfect!"

But when you are being fitted or made up, people are constantly appraising and criticizing you, finding that one flaw in your body or your appearance, then rubbing your nose in it. "Honey," they say, "you've got too much here or not enough there," or, "How are we going to hide this flaw or that imperfection?" They don't intend to be cruel. It's just that they don't view you as a person. You're an object, a mannequin to hang clothes on. It's a job, it's business. But it can emotionally destroy you.

On top of that, I had to be constantly watchful that people were not stealing from me. Some of the other models thought nothing of stealing my bookings. Even the people I hired to look after my finances were taking advantage of me. I started modeling two days after my eighteenth birthday, and suddenly I had more money than I knew what to do with. You don't need much money at eighteen. You truly don't. Living in New York, I didn't even need a car—just an apartment. Everything I needed was just a short walk or cab ride away.

I hired an accountant to handle my business affairs, and he said, "Here, let me help you. I'll invest your earnings and pay all your bills for you. All you have to do is sign this paper so I can have access to your checking account." And trusting teenager that I was, I fell for it. On top of what I paid him, he also helped himself to around $45,000, as near as I can figure.

My parents never pushed me into the modeling business. I never sought it out myself. I was "discovered" in my own hometown while I was minding my own business, going to a local modeling school in Buffalo. But I've met so many young women who were pushed into the modeling business by ambitious parents. I'm often approached by parents who bring their beautiful teenage daughter to me and say, "Don't you think she should be a model? Could you help her get into the business?"

I always look at those kids and say, "Why do you want to work and pay taxes? You're just a kid. Go play. Have fun. Be a kid. You've got plenty of time to grow up and be an adult."

I acquired a lot of money and fame at an early age, and I simply did not know what to do with it or how to manage it. In school, they teach you how to diagram sentences and what an isosceles triangle is, but they don't teach you how to manage money, how to pick a lawyer, how to hire an accountant, or how to stand up for yourself. There were a lot of people who knew I didn't know the difference when it came to finances, and I was taken advantage of.

There were all sorts of upsetting experiences that went with the money and fame of the modeling world. I used to go home to Lockport, tearful, exhausted, needing a break, needing to recover from all the bruising personal critiques and stressful pressures I had been subjected to. But when I arrived home, I was really *home*, I was safe, I was where I belonged, with people who expected nothing of me and were simply glad to see me. My first year in modeling, I had to come home at least once every couple of months just to get back to basics. My "bookers" at the modeling agency would see how stressed out I was getting, and they would compassionately cancel all of my bookings so I could go home and recharge.

I don't know what I would have done without a home to run to—a place of unconditional acceptance, security, and familiarity. It was so nice, after weeks of hotels, restaurants, and airplanes just to be home, lounging in the bedroom or the living room I grew up in, with my mom in the kitchen fixing dinner. It was so comfortable to hear those familiar voices, to breathe in those familiar aromas, to let my guard down and allow my parents to take care of me. After a few days of R and R, I was ready to go back to the battle zone again.

Home Is Better

Early in my modeling career, I had a foot in each world—the small-town, family-oriented world I grew up in and the big-city world of the fashion industry. As I left my teens and grew into my twenties, my perspective slowly changed. I gradually became more accustomed to the fast-paced world of New York and didn't feel I needed the support of family and home as much. It was good that I was becoming more secure and self-sufficient—that's part of maturity.

But what was not so good, as I look back on it, was that I was gradually buying into the worldly mind-set of the modeling world. In time, my viewpoint changed so much that I would go back to Lockport and look around my hometown and see how people dressed and looked and lived—and I would begin to feel rather smug. *These small-town people live in such ignorance and bliss,* I thought. *They are scarcely even aware of the excitement and glamour of the world I live in!* I had begun to see my hometown with tainted eyes.

Instead of thinking, *Gee, it's so nice to be back home,* I'd think, *Gee, I didn't realize how small this house is!* Understand, my father was fairly well off—medium-wealthy, you might say. We always had enough money for nice vacations, we had a little boat for water-skiing, and we lived in a nice house in a cute neighborhood. We didn't live in a mansion, but it wasn't a crackerbox, either. It was just right.

But when I left my little just-right world and entered the modeling world, I was immersed in a fast-lane culture filled with people who lived life at full-throttle. I became surrounded by people who greedily, hungrily gobbled up all the material things, pleasure, and excitement a city like New York had to offer. I was surrounded by people like Gia—people who could never have enough of the good things in life. They could afford the best of everything and the most of everything, and they got it.

I began to love the world I was in—and who wouldn't? Every day, I was on a shoot at some penthouse or exotic location, with fur coats and jewels dripping off me, with armed guards around me because everything I was wearing was worth a king's ransom! The top photographers in the world were snapping their shutters at me, saying, "Oh, you're the most beautiful thing! Gorgeous! You're the best!" Well, that can go to your head in a New York minute.

At the same time, I often experienced a kind of disorientation—a confusing sense of "Who am I?" After I played my part in front of the cameras, after I shed the furs and jewels, after I took off my makeup and put my jeans back on, it was as if I wasn't anybody anymore. I would go back to my apartment and I would read books, and I'd just be Kim from Lockport. If I left my apartment and went out on the street, the deli man would scowl at me, the cabdrivers would yell at me, the doorman would ignore me.

Every day, I'd go out to a different location or a different studio, working with different people, just going wherever the agency sent me. I'd put on the clothes and makeup they wanted me to wear, get into character, and—ta-dah!—I'd be Kim Alexis again. Sometimes it seemed as if there were two Kims—the real me and this role I played, a fantasy existence known as Supermodel Kim Alexis. I'd look at myself in the mirror and wonder, *Why do they call me a "supermodel"? Where does that term come from? There's nothing "super" about me!*

Too much sense of style and sophistication can really skew your perspective—and that's what happened to me. It took me a few years to realize that my fast-lane friends at Studio 54 weren't any happier than those small-town folks I had left behind in Lockport.

Now that I'm in my thirties, I'm much happier because I don't have to be this fantasy supermodel anymore. My public persona and the real me can be one and the same. I can be open about who I really am and what I really believe. And what I've come to realize, as I've matured from a fresh-faced young model starting out in New York into a mother-athlete-spokeswoman, is that *home* and *family* are very important to me. The family values I grew up with in Lockport are very precious to me.

Dancing all night at Studio 54 and jetting all over the world are *fun*—but family is *real* and *lasting*. Family values are an anchor for life.

Today, Ron and I are very comfortable with who we are and how we live. We don't have a jet-set lifestyle and we don't live in an elaborate mansion on a rambling estate. We have a very nice home in southern California, with some sheep, pigs, and goats in the backyard. We've made our home a nice place for our children to live and play, because what's most important to us is *family*. We don't have millions of dollars worth of artwork in our home—we have photos and mementos of our careers and our family memories, because we don't want our house to be a ritzy, artsy museum; we want it to be a nice, warm *home*, a secure and comfortable shelter for our family.

I've been in the fast-lane celebrity world and I've been in the cozy little world of home and hearth and family. I can tell you one thing for sure: Home is better.

Teaching Begins at Home

The best way we can prepare our kids for life is not by teaching them how to have latex sex, but by helping them understand the richness and satisfaction that come from a loving, committed marriage relationship. We need to teach boys to respect girls, and we need to teach girls to respect themselves. We need to teach our kids that their best hope for being happy and fulfilled lies not in casual sex, but in building a strong two-parent family. How do we instill these values in our kids? Here are some suggestions for ways we can raise safe, strong kids—even in this dangerous, kid-unfriendly world:

1. Pray. I continually pray for God's protection around my kids. There is a spiritual war going on in this world, and the enemy has our kids in his crosshairs. I refuse to allow them to be casualties of this battle. I pray that God will daily surround our kids with His spiritual armor. And I also pray daily, "Father, please place a hunger and thirst for spiritual truth within my kids. Please make them always want to be close to You and to have a lasting, loving, personal relationship with You."

2. Let children know they are loved. I really believe that Gia's abandonment at age eleven made her feel unloved and unlovable, and that's why she chased after fame and excitement in the modeling world. So many people who go into modeling, acting, music, politics, and other performing professions are really looking for love and seeking affirmation and a sense of okay-ness from the adulation of the crowds. They think that through becoming a famous celebrity, they will obtain the love and affirmation they were denied in childhood. I was fortunate to know I was loved as a child. It was really the love of my family that anchored my life and kept me from the destructive influences and temptations that destroyed poor Gia.

3. Talk to children openly and honestly about family, sex, character, values, and virtue. Parents are the first, best, and most influential teachers of children, and we should be open and unembarrassed in talking with our kids about sex and morality. That means we have to take time for family talks and one-on-one times with our kids.

4. Model what we teach. We have to go beyond mere words and teach our kids by our lives. That means we make a point of modeling healthy sexual attitudes and behavior. We show our children that their mommy and daddy love each other, are affectionate with each other, cherish each other, and are romantic and appropriately sexual with each other. It's good for our kids to see their parents touching, hugging, kissing, and talking sweetly to each other. It's important for them to see that a committed marriage relationship is beautiful and worth waiting for.

5. *Monitor the media messages that come into the home.* That means we have to be aware of everything our kids are watching and listening to. That means checking the CDs and videos children bring home. That means paying attention to what's on TV and, if necessary, flipping the channel or simply switching off the tube and sending the kids out to play. In the Duguay household, our kids watch TV on weekends, not on school nights (homework always takes precedence over entertainment). If I see my kids watching a TV show that depicts an anti-Christian or occult message, I turn it off, then sit down and talk with my kids about what they've just seen.

On one occasion, for example, my kids were watching a show in which a superhero announces, "I have the power!" and he begins to radiate with an unearthly glow. So I turned off the TV and said, "There are a lot of people in this world who think it's okay to use supernatural powers from evil spirits or from the Force or whatever. But we are Christians, and we believe only in the power that comes from God.

"The Bible says that we are to pray whenever we need help, and then we are to let God answer our prayer in the way and the time He chooses. It's wrong and it's dangerous to use supernatural powers to try to make things go our way or to affect other people." God is the power!

As Christian parents, we are responsible for what comes into our homes and the influence it has on our children's minds. We all have a million things to do, we all get tired, but that is no excuse to park our kids in front of the telenanny. If we use TV as a baby-sitter, there will be a price to pay.

Another source of information and entertainment that is having a major influence on our kids is the Internet. From the keyboard of your home computer, your children can literally access any kind of information from anyplace around the world. With a few keystrokes, your child can download games and music, or research a term paper, or get the latest sports news, or download the vilest, most obscene pornography imaginable, or get instructions on how to build a bomb. The Internet is not good or evil; it is a morally neutral tool, like a VCR or a television. There's a lot that's good on the Web and a lot that's evil. It's our responsibility to make sure our kids use the family computer wisely and safely.

Parents should always monitor and supervise what kids are doing with the computer. This is especially true when our children surf the Net. There is software available at any good computer store to help keep kids out of dangerous Web sites—but be aware that none of these software solutions is foolproof. You, the parent, must still keep an eye on your kids and the computer. It helps to keep the computer in a high-traffic family area, so that kids can be observed and are not left alone with the Internet for long periods of time.

It is also a good idea for parents to check their computers from time to time to see what sites the kids have been visiting. You can do this by opening the "history" folder in your Web browser or by examining the contents of the "Windows/history" or "Windows/temporary Internet files" folders in Microsoft Windows. You will be able to see all the Web sites that have been recently visited by that computer. If you don't know how to check these folders on your computer, have a computer-literate friend help you—and read *Making the Internet Family Friendly* by Brian Lang and Bill Wilson. These days, it pays to know just a little bit more about your computer than your kids know!

It's natural for all boys, at a certain stage of their development, to be curious about things like sex and pornography. But when kids are exposed to such influences at the wrong time in their lives, they can experience lasting damage to their psychological, emotional, and sexual development. So I'm committed to being vigilant about all the various forms of media that come into our home.

6. *Teach kids to memorize Scripture.* God's Word builds character and serves as a vaccination against the moral and spiritual viruses that swirl around our kids throughout each day. It is said that "nature abhors a vacuum," and if we do not fill our kids' minds and hearts with the truth of God's Word, then the destructive lies of this world are sure to rush into that void. God's Word truly is a lamp, lighting the pathway and guiding the footsteps of our children. God's view of marriage and sexual responsibility is found in such passages as Ephesians 5:22–33; 1 Corinthians 6:9–20; 2 Corinthians 6:14; 1 Thessalonians 4:1–8; and 1 Peter 2:11.

7. *Prepare kids to stand up to peer pressure and temptation.* We do this by building our children's self-esteem, so that they feel strong and secure in themselves. We do this by helping them to understand that they don't need to sacrifice their standards in order to be accepted and approved by others. We do this by making sure they feel loved at home, so that they don't need to go chasing after love by giving away their virginity or taking drugs in order to be accepted by the group.

8. *Set standards about the kind of company kids keep.* We need to be aware of exactly *whom* our kids hang out with, *where* they hang out, and *what they do* when they hang out. Children

and teenagers should not be trusted with too much unaccountable time. We should also be aware that bad friends will often lure kids into situations and temptations they might not get into on their own. Parents should not hesitate to break up a friendship that is clearly unhealthy and leading the child astray.

It is especially important for parents to screen their kids' friends when they reach the age at which they begin dating. Parents should always meet their children's dates, and should look for character qualities such as courteousness, respect for self and others, respect for authority, trustworthiness, truthfulness, humility, a well-adjusted personality, a good reputation, and faith in Jesus Christ.

I recently came across an item that's been making the rounds on the Internet—a father's "So-You-Want-to-Date-My-Daughter" application form. Though it was written tongue-in-cheek, having our kids' prospective dates fill out a form like the one on page 106 might not be such a bad idea! It may seem a *little* overly strict—but the principle is clear: Today, more than ever, we need to be aware of whom our kids spend time with, and how they are spending that time.

A pastor friend of mine once said that when he went out on a date, his mother would always tell him, "Remember that Jesus is in the backseat." Having that sense of the Lord's presence with him, he said, helped to keep his dating behavior moral and pure.

Dennis Rainey, host of the *Family Life* radio program, has written an excellent book, *Parenting Today's Adolescent,* which will help many parents navigate the treacherous waters of their child's adolescence.

I came across some lines that were faxed to radio talk show host Dr. Laura Schlessinger, which she posted on her Internet

Web site. Titled "If I Had a Child to Raise Over Again," written by Diane Loomans, these reflections on parenting give me something to ponder as I work to raise children who feel loved, confident, and secure in their own self-image. I can't think of a better way to close this chapter than with these thoughtful lines:

> If I had a child to raise over again,
> I'd fingerpaint more, and point the finger less.
> I'd do less correcting and more connecting.
> I'd take my eyes off my watch and watch with my eyes.
> I would care to know less and know to care more.
> I'd take more hikes and fly more kites.
> I'd stop playing serious and seriously play.
> I'd run through more fields and gaze at more stars.
> I'd do more hugging and less tugging.
> I would be firm but affirm much more.
> I'd build self-esteem first and build the house later.
> I'd teach less about the love of power
> And more about the power of love.[1]

APPLICATION FOR PERMISSION
TO DATE MY DAUGHTER

This application will be incomplete and rejected unless accompanied by a financial statement, job history, ten (10) character references, and current medical report from your doctor.

Name _____

Height _____ Weight _____ IQ _____ GPA _____

Date of Birth _____ Driver's License No._____

Social Security No._____ Boy Scout Rank _____

Home Address _____

Number of years your parents have been married _____

Answer the following questions fully and truthfully (or else):

1. Do you own a van? _____
2. A water bed? _____
3. A truck with oversize tires? _____
4. A tattoo in any size, shape, or form? _____
5. Do you have an ear ring? _____
6. Nose ring? _____
7. Belly-button ring?_____

> (*If you answered yes to any of these seven question, discontinue the application and leave the premises.*)

8. What does "late" mean to you? _____
9. In fifty words or less, what does "Don't touch my daughter" mean to you? _____

10. In fifty words or less, what does "abstinence" mean to you? _____

11. Answer the following questions by filling in the blanks. Please answer freely—all answers are confidential.

11a. If I were shot, the last place in my body I would want to be wounded is in the _____

11b. A woman's place is in the _____

11c. The one thing I hope this application does not ask me about is _____

11d. When I meet a girl, the first thing I notice about her is

_____

_____

(If your answer to 11d. makes reference to anatomical endowments, leave the premises, keep your head low, and run in a serpentine fashion.)

12. What do you want to be IF you grow up? _____

I swear that all information supplied above is true and correct to the best of my knowledge, under penalty of death, dismemberment, Singapore-style caning, and torture by red hot pokers.

Signature _____

Thank you for your interest in dating my daughter. Please allow four to six years for processing of this application. You will be contacted in writing if you are approved. Please do not try to call or write. Have a nice day.

8

Supermodel or Supermom: What's a Career Mother to Do?

I made my acting debut in late 1991 on the set of Stephen J. Cannell's TV cop show, *The Commish*. We shot the episode, entitled "Officer April," over five days in beautiful Vancouver, British Columbia. The cast and crew were wonderful to me and very professional. I was awed by the talent of everyone on the show, and my first day on the set, I thought, *What am I doing here? I'm not an actress—I'm a fish out of water!* But everyone was so kind to me and patient with me that the entire experience ended up being very painless and a lot of fun.

Coming out of the modeling world, I expected to be subjected to constant criticism: "Your dress needs to be an inch lower! Why did you pick *that* out? Ugh, black shoes! Your nylons should be a lighter sheer! And would you just lose those earrings? This is not right at all, we're going to have to change everything!" But on the set of *The Commish*, nobody criticized, everyone was laid back, everyone helped and supported everyone else. It was a pleasure to work in a place where everyone looked for the good in you, not just your flaws.

My next acting job was in the historic final episode of *Cheers,* "One for the Road," which we shot in early 1993. Instead of working on a closed set, as we did on *The Commish,* this show was shot before a live studio audience. Again, I was in awe of where I was. Ron was with me for the filming, and I kept grabbing him by the arm and saying, "Can you believe where I am right now? This is big-time! This is TV history! This is the last episode of one of the top TV shows of all time! Why did God put me here? Why me? How did I get this job?" I had watched the show for years, and it was an incredible thrill for me to step into the lives of the show's characters and to become a part of their world.

"Don't think about all that," Ron said. "Just go out and do it." Ron's practical, straightforward way of handling situations helps to steady me and settle me down.

I played the part of "Supermodel Kim Alexis." And yes, I have to put that in quotes, because every time my name is mentioned in the episode, it's never just "Kim Alexis." It's always "stunning supermodel Kim Alexis." Or "electrifying supermodel Kim Alexis." Or "dazzling supermodel Kim Alexis." It got to be embarrassing after a while.

As the episode opens, Norm, Cliff, and the rest of the Cheers gang are in the bar, watching the Cable Ace awards on TV—and waiting for me to come on to present one of the awards. Cliff, the mailman, says, "Supermodel Kim Alexis—how often her lovely form has graced the pages of the *Sports Illustrated* swimsuit issue!"

Then one of the other bar patrons asks, "Are you sure the dazzling supermodel Kim Alexis is going to be on the show?"

Later, Sam walks in and Norm tells him, "We're breathlessly awaiting the appearance of the stunning supermodel Kim Alexis."

And so it went.

Finally, I come on to present an award for best writing, along with former Chicago Bears head coach Mike Ditka. The coach and I banter a bit—then we announce the winner of the award. The award goes to (of all people) Diane Chambers (Shelley Long, who returns to the show for the final episode). Diane comes up to the podium and gives an interminable and outrageously pretentious acceptance speech, while the coach and I keep checking our watches. Finally, Mike Ditka and I have to physically yank her off the stage.

It was great fun, a real fantasy experience, and I enjoyed meeting all those people I had watched on TV every Thursday night— Rebecca Howe (Kirstie Alley), Woody (Woody Harrelson), Carla (Rhea Perlman), Norm (George Wendt), Frasier Crane (Kelsey Grammer), Cliff Clavin (John Ratzenberger), and the rest. (I didn't get to meet Ted "Sam Malone" Danson, because he was not there for my day of taping.) All the cast members signed a copy of the script and gave it to me, and I have it framed on the wall of my home.

A Delicate Balancing Act

Later that same year, I also appeared in a Perry Mason mystery movie for NBC, "The Case of the Wicked Wives," along with Kathy Ireland, Shelley Hack (the original Charlie perfume girl), and Paul Sorvino. I was pregnant with Noah when we did that show. I played one of the "wicked wives"—though I wasn't *that* wicked (I was a suspect, but not the murderer). The murder victim was a photographer whose ex-wives were three supermodels (Kathy, Shelley, and me) whom he had blackmailed with his photos. I accepted the role because the character I played was not that different from the real me. I don't want to do anything that is too far from my image or that would hurt my image—I really protect this part of me. There are a lot of perfectly nice people who get nasty fan mail because they play villains on TV—so I'd rather portray myself than pretend to be someone else.

The film was shot in Denver, so my mom came out from New York to stay with our kids at the house in southern California. The movie took about three weeks to shoot, and I would work five days, come home for three, then go back. Going back and forth like that, I wasn't away from my children for too long at a time.

Ron came to visit me on the set when we were in the middle of shooting. The day he arrived, the news broke that another of our annual southern California fires, fanned by the Santa Ana winds, was cutting right through our area! I turned on CNN, and sure enough, I instantly recognized the area in the news video. Homes were blazing just a few blocks away from my house! I tried to call home, but the circuits were jammed and my call wouldn't go through. I was frantic!

I don't know how many times I called, but I finally got through and heard my answering machine. *Well,* I figured, *if the answering machine is working, the house must still be standing.* I later found out that when my mother saw the flames, she packed up the children, grabbed our wedding albums and a few other belongings, and went to the house of some friends. Later, my nanny, who was with my mother and the kids, managed to get a call through to her parents in Iowa, who called me and told me everyone was okay.

The point is that there are times when my career takes me away from my home and my kids—sometimes at very crucial moments! At times it is a delicate balancing act, being both a mother and a career woman. It's a balancing act I approach with care, prayer, and an absolute commitment that my family comes first. Yes, my career is very important, but nothing comes ahead of my Lord and my family.

Some mothers can juggle several roles. For example, I've been a mother, a model, an actress, and a spokesperson. I'm a little of this and a little of that—but that's me. There are women who manage even more roles than I do, while others decide that one role at a time is appropriate and right. We each need to make that decision for ourselves.

The feminist movement has made many stay-at-home moms feel inferior, as if they are missing out on something—and that's wrong. We need to honor women who take on the full-time job of raising strong, healthy, secure kids who will make this world a better place. Nurturing children takes more time, work, energy, intelligence, skill, creativity, dedication, and character than almost any other career you could imagine. It's a tragedy of our times that all too many full-time moms cringe with embarrassment when asked, "What do you do for a living?" Women who make the choice and the sacrifice to devote their full time to raising strong, emotionally healthy, spiritually vibrant, decent children should not only be affirmed and applauded—we should put up a statue in the park for each one! (And I include in that group my own mother—thanks, Mom!)

Full-time mom or career mom? It's a purely individual choice, based on individual circumstances. But as we make this choice, we have to recognize that—contrary to what some in our society would have us believe—no one can have it all. I constantly deal with this balancing act, because I have chosen to maintain both a career and my role as a mother. The nature of my work enables me to spend a lot of time with my children—but it also calls me away and requires some sacrifices.

I couldn't do without my role as the mother of my children.

I spend a lot of time with them, talking with them, taking care of them, answering their questions, wiping their runny noses, singing and playing and praying with them, and talking to them about Jesus. But I believe God has also given me the gift of a career and the responsibility to use it wisely. As much as I love both my motherhood role and my career role, I think it would drive me crazy to do just one or the other. That's not for everybody—that's just me.

Since Noah was born, I've been spending a lot more time at home with my kids. I've slowed the pace of my life. I've still been able to accomplish a lot in my career, taping TV shows such as *Your Mind and Body, Parenting in the '90s and Beyond* on CBS, and fitness and nutrition segments on *The 700 Club*. But there's nothing more important to me than making sure my children all have a good base of security, love, affirmation, and Christian instruction.

Whenever I'm offered a job, Ron and I weigh the offer together, considering first of all how that job will impact our family. We pray about it, talk about it, and we always get a good sense of what God wants me to do. If the impact on our family is too great, I turn it down. My agent knows where I stand, what I will do in terms of time commitment, and what my reasons are. He prescreens my job offers, and many projects I'm offered never even reach my hands because my agent knows I would never consider taking that much time away from my family.

We don't have time to do everything in life. There are only so many hours in a day, only so many days in a year, only so many years in a lifetime. You can't have it all. If you work fifty or sixty hours a week, your kids are going to miss you, they're going to suffer—there's no way around it. If you turn your kids over to the lady at the day-care center, then face it: You won't be as close to your children as the lady at the day-care center. You will lose some of that special time with your children, and you will never get it back.

In our society, we work harder so we can have more toys, and the more toys we have, the more money we must make to keep up our toys. You may remember the bumper sticker that read, "The one who dies with the most toys wins." To some people, that's funny—and that's their view of life. To me, that's an expression of a completely meaningless existence. My life is not about acquiring toys, acquiring things, acquiring money or status. My life is about spending time with my family and with my Lord. That is where true meaning and satisfaction in life are found.

Many women have discovered that working outside the home is really a false economy—by the time they add up the cost of day care, transportation, a business wardrobe, eating out, and being kicked into a higher tax bracket, they discover they are actually *losing money* by being employed! The Children's Defense Fund says that one-third of all children of working mothers are either poor or would be poor if Mom didn't work outside the home. So there are situations where the need to be employed is very real. But the flip side of that statistic is that *two-thirds* of working mothers could afford *not* to work. It might require an economic sacrifice to stay at home, but they could do it. For most mothers, it's a choice, not a necessity—and that's something to think about.

I believe the answer for many families is that, instead of sending Mom out to the workforce, they should learn to live more simply and inexpensively as a family. As a culture, we've bought into the notion that acquiring a career or status or material things will make us happy. TV tells us buy, buy, buy, spend, spend, spend, and you'll be happy—and we buy the message and spend the money, but are we happier? (Since I'm a spokeswoman on several commercials, I'm part of the advertising culture I'm talking about—and I take my responsibility seriously. That's why I try to represent only products that are important, worthwhile, and worthy of people's hard-earned dollars.)

We've lost track of what *truly* makes us happy. The fact is, spending intimate time with God and family is what truly generates happiness, meaning, and lasting satisfaction in our lives. We're so busy running around like little ants that we never stop to listen and hear what the Spirit of God has to say to us: *Slow down. Be still. Simplify your life. Find your satisfaction in Me, not things.*

Ron and I could buy a lot of things and do a lot of things we don't choose to buy or do. We live near L.A., and we could do the L.A. celebrity scene every night of the week, but that's not where our values are.

The "Day-Care Crisis"

There are some people in this country who say there is a "day-care crisis" in America. They say we need more federal tax dollars to subsidize more day care for the children of working families. But there are others in our country who are looking at this issue from a different perspective and asking, "Wouldn't it be better if parents didn't *have* to put their children into day-care facilities? Wouldn't it be better if kids could be raised in families instead of in federally subsidized day-care centers?"

According to the nonpartisan Tax Foundation, American breadwinners in 1998 had to work from January 1 to May 10 just to pay their taxes. It hasn't always been this way. In 1913 a worker had to work only from January 1 to January 30 to pay taxes; after that, he and his family could keep, save, invest, and spend everything else he earned. In 1925, the tax bite took from January 1 to February 6 to pay. In the 1950s and early 1960s, workers had to labor from January 1 to about April 1 just to pay taxes. Today, American families are forced to spend more on taxes than on shelter, food, clothing, and transportation *combined*. No wonder it's so difficult for families to make it on one paycheck! I'm reminded of the bumper sticker that says, "God only asks 10 percent—why does Uncle Sam take half?"

What if, instead of subsidizing more institutions to warehouse children of working families, we gave that money back to the families who earned it in the first place? What if we let people keep more take-home pay so that mothers could afford to stay home with their kids? The best place for children to be cared for is in the family, not in a center or a facility. Look, I don't claim to be an expert on social policy or taxation, but to me, it's just a matter of common sense: Let's make it affordable once more—as it was in the days of Donna Reed and June Cleaver—for mothers to take care of their kids full-time, if that's what they choose. Women should be permitted to have careers, if they choose—but women should also be permitted to stay home with their kids. They should not be forced by high taxation to join the workforce against their will and against their nurturing instinct.

According to *The Los Angeles Times,* the proportion of mothers with infants and toddlers in the paid workforce has climbed from 25 percent in 1965 to 65 percent in the late 1990s. And the U.S. Census Bureau says that only 17 percent of American households today fit the traditional model of a breadwinning father, a homemaking mother, and one or more kids.[1]

While more American kids than ever before are spending

their quality time in day care, the latest research shows that the quality of care in these institutional settings is dangerously low. A 1995 study entitled "Cost, Quality, and Child Outcomes in Child Care Centers," conducted by researchers from Yale, UCLA, the University of Colorado, and the University of North Carolina at Chapel Hill, has found that of one hundred day-care centers surveyed, only one out of seven provided a level of quality that promoted learning and healthy development. The study found that child care in most centers was "poor to mediocre," and fully 40 percent of babies and toddlers received a "less than minimal" level of care. Only 14 percent of the centers surveyed offered "high-quality care," as defined in terms of "high staff-to-child ratios, more highly educated staff, administrators with more experience, and staff stability."[2] What these facts show is that, on the whole, the quality of institutional day care is so abysmal, it should be avoided if at all possible.

Danielle Crittenden, cofounder of the Independent Women's Forum, points out that there is something disastrously wrong when, in a nation as rich as the United States, mothers are driven into the workplace by economic necessity. "In the space of a generation," she told *The L.A. Times,* "have we come to consider taking care of your own kids—even if it's just for the few short years before they are in school—as a perk of the rich, like yachting?"[3]

Yes, there is a day-care crisis in America—and the crisis is simply that there are too many kids in day care! You may be one of those mothers who is forced, reluctantly and unhappily, to place your children in some form of "other-than-mother" care. You may be a single mother or even a mother in a two-parent family, and after doing all the calculations, you realize that you have absolutely no choice but to place your kids in a day-care center. If that is your situation right now, please don't feel judged or criticized. Don't feel that you have failed. You do what you have to in order to get by and to take care of your family. I affirm you in that.

If you absolutely have to resort to some form of "other-than-mother" care for your children, you can still make the best of a tough situation. Here are some suggestions:

1. *Seek creative options and alternatives.* You may be a single mother, maintaining a job and an apartment, struggling from paycheck to paycheck, paying legal bills, trying to get your ex-husband to make child-support payments on time. Have you thought of moving back with your parents? Sure, it may feel demeaning, you may lose that sense of autonomy and personal freedom you gained when you first moved out—but what really counts now is what's best for your kids. Wouldn't it be better to surround your kids with family, with grandparents and maybe an aunt or uncle or two, instead of putting them in "stranger-care"? It would also cut your expenses at a time when money is very dear.

Other creative alternatives: Trade baby-sitting chores with other parents (which can work well if you have a creative work situation, such as job sharing, flextime, working at home, or telecommuting). Or take your baby to work (some bosses and companies will let you keep a child in the same room or a nearby room—which is especially nice for breast-feeding mothers).

2. *Listen to your hunches, feelings, and the Spirit's voice.* When you check out a child-care situation, you have to use your intellect and do your homework—but you also should listen to your feelings. When something is not quite right about a situation, I often get a sick feeling deep inside. I may not be able to put my finger on what's wrong about the situation, but that sick feeling tells me that *something* is wrong. We should never guide our lives entirely by our feelings—but we should

not ignore our God-given feelings, either. Sometimes, the facts and figures of a situation may all look good, but there is a hidden problem that our intellect cannot see. So we must rely upon the Spirit of God to enlighten us and warn us when there are hidden dangers. When He speaks to us in that still, small voice, we need to listen and obey.

3. Have a contingency plan. Make sure your care provider knows what to do if you are late to pick up your child. And make sure your care provider knows who has permission to pick up your child and—more important, in cases of divorce and custody disputes—who does not. Keep your caregiver informed of anything that is going on in your home that might affect your child—the death of a pet or family member, separation or divorce, a move, a change in a parent's job situation, and so forth.

4. Be aware of your child's feelings, especially anxiety about separation. If possible, gradually introduce your child to the new care provider. Let them spend an hour a day together, while you are present, so that your child will get to know and trust the new person. Bring toys and other familiar items that will help your child feel secure in the new setting. Before leaving your child, spend time with her, reading or playing together, trading hugs and kisses. Make sure your child understands you will be back at a certain specific time, such as, "after your nap." Avoid the temptation to sneak away while the child is not looking—this can damage trust, even if the child seems absorbed in some activity. Instead, try to build a good-bye tradition, make it part of the daily routine—a kiss, a big hug, a prayer, a promise to return, a wave, and a smile. Instead of telling your child not to cry, say, "I know you don't want me to go, but I'll be back after I finish my work and then we'll have fun together." Accept your child's feelings—don't deny them.

5. *Reduce morning stress.* Avoid rushing your child; wake him early enough to have some "fiddle-around" time before the day begins. If possible, give yourself some time so the two of you can "fiddle around" together. Have the child's clothes and take-along toys laid out the night before. If you and your child have trouble getting off on time, set an alarm (or a series of alarms!) to warn you at increments before it's time to head out the door.

6. *Reduce evening stress.* At the end of the day, take some time to give your children your full attention. After you pick them up, use the drive time to reconnect, ask questions, share feelings, and laugh together. When you get home, take time to talk to your children, listen to them, and look them in the eye and nod as they tell you about their day. Ooh and aah over their drawings and papers. Laugh at their jokes. When you ask them about their day, don't ask questions that can be answered "yes," "no," or "fine." Ask for specific information that has to be explained: "Tell me one thing you learned today. Tell me one thing that made you laugh today. What was the most fun thing you did today? What was the yuckiest thing that happened today?" Relate your child's experiences to your own childhood: "I used to like playing four-square when I was your age too."

After spending time with your kids, take a little time to relax, listen to music, exercise, take a walk, unwind, decompress, read, pray. Avoid stressful activities or emotions—try not to criticize or yell or nag your kids right after you get home. Give your children simple, manageable chores to involve them in the family ritual and to lighten your load— chores such as setting the table or helping with dinner. Begin the meal with prayer, and throughout the meal, share stories and feelings, and keep mealtime conversation pleasant, upbeat, and loving. Never end the evening without a time of prayer and family devotions, including a brief Bible story from a children's devotional book.

7. Make time for romance and relationship with your mate. Take time every evening to talk and reconnect. Both of you should set a goal of sharing joys and frustrations from the day, and affirming each other's feelings. At least once a month, leave the kids with friends or grandparents so the two of you can go out to dinner or have a romantic evening at home.

8. Let your kids into your world. Take your children to work with you every once in a while so that they can see what you do every day while they are in day care or school. Tell your children that this is how you make money so that you can take care of your family, so that they can have good food, a nice house, warm clothes, medical care, and other things they need every day. Help your children to see that the work you do is an act of love for your family.

9. Keep baby-sitters posted on house rules. When you have a baby-sitter, keep a card prominently displayed (say, on the refrigerator) with emergency numbers, numbers of friends and grandparents, and house rules regarding meals and snacks, behavioral guidelines, bedtime, television shows (which shows are allowed, which are forbidden), use of computer and video games, and so forth. Clear, posted rules can prevent a lot of arguments between the sitter and the child. Make sure your sitter knows that he has been hired to do a job—baby-sitting is not a party or a date, so no boyfriends or girlfriends allowed.

The Shepherd and the Little Sheep

I'm a career mother, and I truly enjoy the "career" side of that label—but I enjoy the "mother" side even more. On those occasions when my work takes me out of town, I want nothing more than to arrive back home and be hit from three sides by big boy hugs! I live for those moments. Nothing beats being home.

After the welcoming hugs, we usually go to the backyard and fall into our big hammock. The kids and I enjoy just lying around, swinging in that hammock, watching our animals grazing on the hill behind our house. To some people, that may not sound like it's as much fun as a trip to Disneyland or a Caribbean cruise, but those are really the moments when my kids and I are the happiest. Those are the moments when we feel grounded, close, together, and secure. We feel connected to each other and to God, and that's what *family* is all about.

It's not easy being a career mother and juggling roles and schedules—but we are not alone in our struggles. As we work hard to shepherd our little lambs, we have the Great Shepherd beside us. Yes, life can be stressful and chaotic—but we can always find green pastures and still waters when we take time to follow our Great Shepherd wherever He leads.

9
A World of Equals

I was once out to dinner with some wealthy friends in Florida. During the meal, the waiter came around and refilled our water glasses. As he filled mine, I said, "Thank you." No big deal, I always thank people when they do something nice for me.

But the man sitting across from me said, "You don't have to thank those people! You're better than they are."

I was shocked! I had never in my life thought of myself as better than anyone else. "God made all of us," I said. "That waiter is just as important as I am. It's just common courtesy to say thank you when someone does something nice for you."

The man looked at me as if I were speaking in another language, as though he could not even comprehend what I had just said. "Really, Kim!" he said, shaking his head at (so he thought) my utter naïveté. "Don't you understand? That guy gets paid minimum wage to fill people's water glasses! You're on the cover of *Vogue* and *Sports Illustrated!* You've done so much more than people like that! Of course you're better than they are! You should realize who you are!"

That conversation was a real eye-opener to me. Since then, I've encountered many people who consider themselves better than others—and I find that completely baffling. Aren't we all God's children? Aren't we all equal in His sight? These same people who claim that some *people* are better than others would undoubtedly be horrified by a claim that some *races* are better than others. Why is racism wrong while me-ism is okay?

Well, racism and me-ism are *both* wrong. And many of the problems in our society today—from crime to political strife to world wars—can be traced directly to the evil of arrogance and inflated egos. It's a me-first attitude that pulls a gun or runs another driver off the road in an act of "road rage." It's a me-first attitude and a disregard for the personhood of others that enable a thief to hit you over the head and take your wallet. It's a me-first attitude that causes one politician to lie and destroy the reputation of another politician. It was a me-first attitude of monstrous arrogance that led Hitler to launch World War II, and that led Sadaam Hussein to take over Kuwait. And it's the same me-first attitude we display when we stand around the office watercooler and damage reputations with gossip.

To See Ourselves as God Sees Us

It's ironic: This man in Florida said I was "better" than other people because my face got me on the covers of so many magazines. Yet for most of my adolescence, I considered my appearance a drawback. I actually grew up feeling punished for being beautiful. My sister, Rhonda, who is very pretty and very intelligent, felt the same way. The kids at school and in the neighborhood didn't want to play with us, and summers were often long and lonely. (I know, I know—"Poor Kim," you say!)

Once, in my early teens, I asked my dad why the kids avoided us, and he said, "Well, honey, it's because you're beautiful. The boys won't ask you out in high school because they're intimidated, they're afraid you're going to say no."

I thought that was so unfair! "I don't want to be beautiful!" I said. "I just want to be popular!"

People think that beauty is a free ticket to happiness, but the fact is, nobody gets a free ticket. Everybody has to deal with something. Some people are too fat, others too skinny, some have to wear glasses, some have chronic health problems, some grow up in poverty, some grow up rich but are shunted off to boarding schools and raised by strangers. All kids grow up with insecurities. No matter what shape we come in, it is a natural human tendency to focus on our faults and weaknesses, and to forget or discount our God-given strengths and advantages.

Equality with Diversity

I rejoice in the fact that there are people who are different from me, who can do things I can't. And I'm very glad there are things I can do that others can't. If everyone else could do what I can do, then who would need me? I'd be out of a job! And let me tell you, there are a lot of people I rely on in the course of a week—the plumber, the mechanic, the airline pilot, the photographer. If I could do my own plumbing, fix my own car, fly my own airplane, and take pictures of myself, all those people would be out of a job!

So we all need one another. We need one another's uniqueness, one another's individual personalities, abilities, creativity, and ideas. While we are all equal, we are all diverse—and our rich human diversity is a beautiful, God-given thing.

In the New Testament, there is a teaching that shows us how God designed human equality and human diversity to work together. This teaching is called "spiritual gifts." In such places as Romans 12; 1 Corinthians 12; Ephesians 4; 2 Timothy 1:6; and 1 Peter 4:11, God's plan for the church is revealed: Through His Spirit, God has given each member of His church different spiritual roles to perform. Although everyone in the church is equal, each person has a unique function to carry out. These roles or spiritual gifts include pastors, teachers, evangelists, administrators, and special abilities of discernment, faith, healing, serving, knowledge, miracles, prophesy, wisdom, tongues, giving, exhorting, encouraging, leading, mercy, and more.

According to the Bible, every Christian believer has one or more spiritual gifts, whether that Christian is young, old, rich, poor, attractive, plain, famous, anonymous, outgoing, or quiet. Some are called to a public ministry; others are gifted with a behind-the-scenes role. Each gift is unique; each person is irreplaceable. When everybody discovers and uses her gift in the church, then the church functions as God intended it to, working harmoniously and accomplishing great things in the world for God.

So no one in the church can say, "I'm not important. I'm a nothing, a zero, a goose egg." Everyone is important. Everyone is unique and has a crucial role to play. We are all parts of a body—fingers, eyes, ears, heart, lungs, bones—and all parts work together to make one functional body. All parts are equal and vital within this rich and diverse living entity called the Christian church.

Jesus created the church to accomplish many purposes: to demonstrate His character and love in the world; to spread the story of His love throughout the world; and to demonstrate to the world how equality and diversity are intended to function perfectly together. Christians are intended to live out the teachings of Jesus, such as the golden rule: "Therefore, whatever you want men to do to you, do also to them, for this is the Law and the Prophets."[1]

Jesus taught us that we are all equals. We treat everyone else as the equal of ourselves. We respect, love, and serve one another, because all our brothers and sisters are the equals of ourselves.

I have never actually counted them up, but I am told that there are fifty-nine "one another" commands in the New Testament, including twenty-one that say, "Love one another." Here is a short synopsis:

"Love one another." (John 13:34; 15:12, 17; Rom. 13:8; 1 Thess. 4:9; 1 John 3:11, 23; 4:7, 11, 12; 2 John 5 NKJV)

"Live in harmony with one another." (Rom. 12:16 NIV).

"Accept one another." (Rom. 15:7 NIV)

"Carry each other's burdens." (Gal. 6:2 NIV)

"Be kind and compassionate to one another." (Eph. 4:32 NIV).

"In humility consider others better than yourselves." (Phil. 2:3 NIV)

"Forgive whatever grievances you may have against one another." (Col. 3:13 NIV)

"Comfort one another." (1 Thess. 4:18; 5:11 NKJV)

"Exhort one another." (Heb. 3:13 NKJV)

"Confess your trespasses to one another." (James 5:16 NKJV)

"Pray for one another." (James 5:16 NKJV)

Every act of human kindness and decency—from a simple "thank you" for a glass of water to the abolition of slavery and oppression—is embodied in that simple biblical prescription: "Love one another."

The Source of Our Confidence as Individuals

My husband, Ron, is a totally confident and comfortable person. He's especially at home on the ice. The moment he steps onto a rink, he just flies. It's an ability God gave him, it's what he loves to do, and he's absolutely wonderful at it. Ron is confident because he's doing what God designed and prepared him to do.

I'm a confident person too. There are things I'm good at, and things I'm not good at. I try to know my own strengths and my own limitations. I'm a great mother. I spend most of my time mothering my kids, and even when I'm away from home, I carry on my mothering role. I call and talk to the kids about their homework, I talk to them about their joys and problems, and I pray with them.

I'm also artistic and musical—I did a lot of music and art in high school, though I put it on the shelf for my kids. I'd love to go back and study music and art again when my children are grown.

I'm good in front of a TV camera. I can do live TV, with or without a TelePrompTer. I enjoy it, and I get better and better at it the more I do it. This is where God put me, this is what I do. And I've learned that I'm at my best when I get myself and my mind and my ego out of the way, and just let God's Spirit flow through me. But I haven't always been this comfortable and confident on TV. First, I had to be dragged out of my comfort zone.

By October 1987, when James was about a year and a half

old, I had been a model for ten years, and my first husband and I owned a group of health clubs in Florida. To help promote the health clubs, I taped some TV spots that aired locally in Florida. I also became a fitness reporter for a local TV station for nine months, and we taped the segments at the health clubs. At the same time, I was looking to get into other areas besides modeling (I knew I couldn't be a model forever), so I went to New York to shop for a new agent. There, I talked to the people at the William Morris agency and I showed them tapes of the TV spots I did in Florida.

"You have a good on-camera presence," they told me. "ABC's *Good Morning America* is looking for a fashion editor, and you'd be perfect. Are you interested?"

Well, I wasn't sure. This was the first time I had been faced with a new career choice since I got out of high school. It would be a huge jump from taping little local spots to going on live, coast-to-coast TV! This was the big time! I was intrigued by the possibilities.

So I went to ABC and met with the producers. They took me on a tour of the offices and studios, and we sat down and talked about what the job would entail. The more I thought about doing live network TV, the colder my feet got. I thought, *I can't do this—I'm going to say no.* Finally, Sonya, one of the producers, said, "So, are you ready? Would you like to join our family at *Good Morning America?*"

I wanted to say, "Are you kidding? I can't do this!" But for some reason that I will never understand, that's not what I said at all. Instead I replied, "I'd love to!" I couldn't believe it! I had taken the job! Well, at least I'd have a few weeks of preparation to get used to the idea, right? Wrong!

Sonya said, "Terrific! You'll begin tomorrow morning at 7:30. What do you plan to wear for your first show?"

Outside, I was smiling. Inside, I was thinking, *What have I done?!* I hardly slept at all that night.

But I made a fascinating discovery in the process of doing *Good Morning America:* Just dive right in and everything will be okay. I've learned to just hold my breath and go for it. That was the beginning of a whole new career on television—and it all happened because I said yes when inside I felt like saying no.

For the next three years, I was *Good Morning America's* fashion correspondent on a once-a-week basis. I got to travel to different places with a camera crew, interview designers, show how designer gowns and furs are made, and more. But even more important, I learned *a lot* about television. Producer Ann Reynolds spent a lot of time with me, showing me how to conduct a live interview, how to bridge from question to question, how to check my notes and prepare my next question when the camera is not on me, how to elicit sound bites from the person I'm interviewing, how to edit my thoughts to fit a tight time slot—all the nuances of my new job.

Everyone was very gracious to me, and I soon felt that I was accepted on my merits—I wasn't as polished a pro as Joan Lunden or Charlie Gibson, but at least I was okay at what I did. And over time, I learned and improved. Now I'm glad I said yes when my insides were screaming no.

So here is one of the great truths I've learned in life, a truth I try to teach my children, a truth I hope you'll take away from our conversation together in this book: Confidence comes from moving out of our comfort zones and taking risks. Confidence comes from holding our breaths and diving right in. Confidence comes from doing the things we fear—and conquering them.

As human beings, we are all wonderful, equal, unique, capable, creative, made in God's image, able to achieve things we can't even imagine until we try. As Christians, we have access to God's limitless resources through prayer and the Holy Spirit. We are all different, all special, all uniquely designed for our own special purpose in life.

As a Christian parent, I want my children to discover their own unique reasons for living, their own special abilities, gifts, and functions to carry out God's plan for their lives—whether that means being a waiter, being a hockey player, or being president of the United States. As long as my children are doing what God has gifted and prepared them to do, I'll be pleased.

10
Defending Life
in a Dying World

I began running marathons in the mid-1980s.

I was getting so sick of seeing all the phony exercise articles in glamour magazines like *Elle* and *Mademoiselle*. I'm talking about articles with titles like "Supermodels' Weight Control Secrets" or "Five Top Supermodels Talk About Staying in Shape" or "Supermodel Thighs—How They Do It." I knew what most readers of these magazines didn't know—that most models don't need to do much of anything to stay in shape.

These magazines would call a famous model and ask, "What do you do to stay in shape?" And she would reply, "Well, I think I did some sit-ups once . . ." And the magazine would turn that into an article! I would see those magazines and know that most of these models were eating burgers and fries, smoking cigarettes, getting zero exercise, and they still looked great. They were just born skinny, that's all.

I always saw myself as more of an athlete than a model. I was a competitive swimmer in high school, and I was very fit and competitive. During school, I swam as many as five hours a day, kept up my studies, was in honor society all through school, and still managed to hold down a part-time job, working in a drugstore for $1.98 an hour. On top of that, I played clarinet in the concert band and marching band, and I was very active in my church youth group. I was always very busy and very athletic when I was young, and I just carried that level of activity into my modeling years and beyond.

In January of 1985 I ran my first marathon in Jacksonville, Florida. My coach, trainer, and encourager was a man named Hank, whom I met through my first husband. Hank had flown into town to run this marathon and wanted me to run part of it with him. I planned to go half the distance, but I got caught up in his excitement and decided the night before the race to attempt the entire distance. Though I had never run anything like a 26.2-mile marathon before, Hank believed in me and said, "Atta girl! Give it a try!"

Hank ran right alongside me as we ran the marathon together. I'd hear him saying as we passed each marker, "Okay, this is only a 5K—you and I can do this." Then, "Okay, we've got the 10K marker coming up, that's just six miles. We've done this plenty of times." I'd moan, "Hank, my feet hurt!" And he was always so positive: "Hey, we're doing great!" To this day, whenever I run, I can hear Hank's voice in my ear, urging me to keep going, we can do this.

When I ran that first marathon in Jacksonville, Hank and I crossed the finish line hand in hand. We did it in four hours, twenty-one minutes. It was one of the toughest, most punishing feats I had ever attempted, but I finished—and just as Hank predicted I would, I had the most wonderful feeling about myself when I completed that first marathon. One of the reasons I was so eager to run marathons was that no other model would do it. I thought it was a good way to prove that I was a real athlete.

Not long after the Jacksonville marathon, a man from the New York City Road Runners Club called me and said, "Would you like to run in the New York City Marathon?" I readily agreed—though I had to drop out before the race when I became pregnant with my first child. James was born in April of 1986, and I ran the marathon the next year when James was just six months old.

A few years later, when I was pregnant with my second child, I agreed to run in the New York City Marathon again—and to be the spokesperson for that event. It seemed like a good idea at the time. I would have my baby, then I would have a few months to get my body back in shape for the marathon. But after Bobby was born, I began to realize that it was not going to be so easy to get back into marathon condition. The closer the date of the race got, the more pressure I felt. *Oh, Kim! I thought. What have you done? It wasn't enough you had to agree to run a marathon after having a baby—you had to stick your neck out and be the spokesperson as well!*

Every day, as I went out and trained for that marathon, I thought, *What I really need right now is a cop-out. Maybe I could just fall and break my ankle, and I wouldn't have to embarrass myself in front of all those people.* I wanted to quit, but I didn't quit—and the biggest reason I kept going was Hank. He believed I could do it, and I didn't want to disappoint his faith in me.

It turned out Hank was right. I did well and finished the race.

Some years later, Hank was diagnosed with cancer. He was treated for it, and he got better. Then the cancer returned.

A Final Visit

I remember one time after Ron and I were married, Ron, Hank, and I were in a restaurant with some other friends. Hank had married a friend of mine, Jody, and Ron and I had gone to Florida to visit them and do a charity event in Jacksonville. He seemed very strong and healthy. We were having a lot of laughs together.

At one point, however, Hank leaned over and said very quietly, so only I could hear, "Kim, it's all through me." And that's all he said about the cancer. Then he leaned back and rejoined the conversation. It was as if he wanted me to know the cancer was serious, but he didn't want to dwell on the negative. He was always such a positive person.

That was in May of 1995, and though I didn't realize it then, it was the last time I would see Hank alive. He was only fifty years old.

Hank was not a Christian believer most of his life, but late in life he came to love Jesus. He talked a lot about Jesus before he died. After I learned that his condition was terminal, I packed up a tape player and a lot of Christian tapes and sent them to his home in Arkansas. I told Jody, "Play these tapes in his room twenty-four hours a day—just let him hear Christian music all the time."

Hank never believed he was going to die. He always thought he was going to beat the cancer and get better, even when his six-foot-two frame was down to ninety pounds and he couldn't walk anymore. I talked with him a number of times on the phone just before he died, and he always told me, "I'm going to get back out and run again."

Around Christmastime of 1995, I was in a sound booth in a studio in L.A., recording some radio spots. I had about twenty scripts, each about two minutes long. A studio sound booth is very quiet, like a prayer chapel, and as I was recording the spots, I had the strongest impression that Hank was there in the booth with me, standing right behind me, watching me work. It was such a strong impression that I turned around and looked, but no one was there. It was a very clear impression—not just a vague impression of *someone,* but a very strong, specific sense that it was *Hank* himself. I hadn't been thinking about Hank at all—I had been concentrating totally on those radio scripts. The experience lasted about ten or fifteen minutes.

It took me about an hour or so to tape the spots. When I got out of the sound booth, I called Ron and asked, "Is there something going on? I just had the strangest feeling about Hank."

"Yeah," Ron replied. "Jody just called. Hank died about an hour ago."

About an hour ago. Right when I felt him there. I don't know anything about such things, but it was nice to have that sense of saying good-bye, because we had been such good friends. He got me into marathon running and taught me a lot about good nutrition, and most of all, he taught me how a person of faith and courage faces life's final test.

Even now, I sometimes find myself talking to Hank when I'm out running, just as I did when we used to run together. I don't ever get the same strong impression of his presence, but sometimes when I'm running, I'll say, "Hank, I'm running this lap for you," or, "Gee, Hank, isn't it hot out today?"

I think about him, and what a vital, active, optimistic man he was, how passionate he was about living life to the fullest, and I find it hard to believe that he was only given fifty years in which to live. But then, when you think of it, even ninety or a hundred years is too short a time to experience everything life has to offer. And what about those who don't even get as much time to live as Hank got—those who die of multiple sclerosis in their thirties or forties, or who die of AIDS in their twenties, or are killed by a drunk driver as children or teenagers? And what about those who are aborted before they even get a chance to experience life outside the womb?

Life is a precious, fragile, priceless thing. Yet we treat it so carelessly and thoughtlessly. We waste it. We pour it out on the ground. We make selfishness our god, and we sacrifice human life on the altar of choice. Life is sacred—and all too brief. We owe it to ourselves and to God to live our lives fully, to use life wisely, to treat life as sacred, and to defend and protect the right to life of others, whether old, young, or unborn.

"A Person's a Person, No Matter How Small"

I'm told that, during a medical convention, a lecturer once posed a situation to a group of physicians in a workshop on the ethics of abortion. He said, "A patient has come to you for medical help and your professional advice. She is a young woman in her early thirties, and she is pregnant for the fourth time. Looking over her medical history, you see that she suffers from tuberculosis, and her health is only fair at best. Her first three pregnancies produced one child who is blind and two others who are deaf. The woman has confided to you that the family lives in poverty because her husband, an alcoholic musician, squanders what little he makes on booze and women. You notice in her medical history that she has previously come to you for treatment of syphilis, which she contracted from her husband. A few months pregnant, she now comes to you and asks: 'Doctor, should I abort this baby or should I give birth?' How would you answer her?"

The doctors in the workshop were informally polled, and 90 percent of them recommended abortion.

"Ladies and gentlemen," the lecturer replied, "you have just voted to abort the great composer, Ludwig van Beethoven."

Since abortion on demand was legalized by the *Roe v. Wade* Supreme Court decision in 1973, some thirty-five million babies have been aborted in America. Today, nearly one in five pregnancies in America is terminated by an abortion procedure. How much great music, literature, and art has been lost because of the loss of those millions of innocent lives? How many times has God sent to us the one who would find the cure for cancer or AIDS, only to see that life aborted before it was ever lived?

Decades of pro-choice propaganda have produced a generation of people who believe that freedom of choice is more important than a right to life. The result is a callous, brutal society, indifferent to the death of innocent human beings. Even though it is politically correct to deny that an unborn baby is really a human life, people instinctively know that a baby isn't magically transformed from nonlife to life by passing through the birth canal. Even though pro-abortion advocates would have us believe that an unborn baby is nothing but a clump of cells, we all know, however much we try to deny it, that if it's not a baby, you're not pregnant. If you're pregnant, it's a baby.

And since society says it's okay to kill a baby in the womb, it's just a short step to concluding that it's okay to kill or abuse a child outside of the womb. That is why we are seeing such horrors as teen mothers who leave their newborn infants in a public toilet or a Dumpster. That is why, since *Roe v. Wade*, the number of reported child abuse cases has increased by *1,497 percent*, from 167,000 in 1973 to 2.5 million in 1991 (according to the U.S. Department of Health and Human Services). By enshrining violence against unborn children as a "right" in America, we have encouraged and contributed to violence against children after they are born.

Do I support a woman's right to choose? You bet I do! Once a child is conceived and a new life has been brought forth in the womb, a woman can choose to keep and lovingly raise her child—or she can lovingly place her child for adoption in an intact, two-parent home. But how can anyone support a "right" or a "choice" to kill an innocent life?

An unborn baby is a separate, distinct human being, even if it is inside a mother's body. That child is not just an "unviable tissue mass" or just "part of the woman's body," like an appendix or tonsils. The instant an egg and sperm join, a distinct human life is formed, with a unique genetic makeup different from the mother's genetic makeup. In half of all pregnancies, the unborn baby is even a different sex from the mother! The baby and mother do not share the same bloodstream—the placenta keeps the mother's blood completely separate from the baby's circulatory system.

By day forty, the baby's brain waves can be detected (doctors consider detectable brain waves and heartbeat to be unmistakable signs of life—they don't "pull the plug" on a patient on life support with brain waves, so why should they "pull the plug" on an unborn baby with brain waves?). After twenty-one days, the heart is beating, and the spinal cord, brain, and nervous system have been formed. By week eight, every organ found in a fully developed adult is functioning—heart, lungs, stomach, kidneys, liver, everything. At this stage, the unborn baby responds to touch and can feel pain. By week thirteen, the baby has fingerprints, can swallow, and fine hair and sex organs have appeared. By week sixteen to eighteen, the baby can hear her mother's voice and heartbeat. By week twenty-four, the baby can survive outside the womb.

Even so, the laws of the United States say that baby can be killed—right up until the moment of her birth! Well, as that great philosopher Dr. Seuss wrote in *Horton Hears a Who,* "A person's a person, no matter how small."

You and I have a responsibility before God to speak up for the innocent in our society who are being led to slaughter. The Bible says,

> Deliver those who are drawn toward death,
> And hold back those stumbling to the slaughter.
> If you say, "Surely we did not know this,"
> Does not He who weighs the hearts consider it?
> He who keeps your soul, does He not know it?[1]

So what is the answer? What is our response? Should we fight fire with fire, fight death with death? Should we try to save unborn lives by bombing abortion clinics? Of course not. Two wrongs never add up to a right.

But we can speak. We can raise our voices in prayer, and we can raise our voices in a national dialogue over abortion. The Supreme Court made a horrendous, tragic error in 1973—an error that has cost thirty-five million innocent lives. But that error can be reversed.

We can support pro-life candidates for public office. We can talk to our friends and neighbors, and stop being ashamed and intimidated about being on the side of life. Yes, in today's society you are not considered cool or hip or politically correct if you favor life over "choice." This is especially true of the entertainment world, where I make my living. When you speak out against abortion in the liberal meccas of New York and L.A., you can expect to be jeered and ridiculed right off the stage. But we can't let that stop us or shut us up. We have to speak the truth, regardless of the cost.

Ultimately, if we who cherish life over choice are vocal enough, passionate enough, caring enough, reasoned enough, and compelling enough, our argument will begin to penetrate the consciousness and conscience of our society. Hearts will change. And when hearts begin to change, laws begin to change.

That is how we build a better future—not by shouting down our opponents, but by changing human hearts.

"The Playgrounds Are Empty . . ."

You may not know who Norma McCorvey is, but you've heard of her. Some years ago, she completely changed the political and social landscape of America. For many years, she was known only as "Jane Roe"—the Roe of the disastrous Supreme Court decision *Roe v. Wade.* Though she herself has never had an abortion, it was her case that led to the decision that legalized abortion on demand in all fifty states.

Norma McCorvey was born in 1947, in Lettesworth, Louisiana, north of Baton Rouge, the child of an absent father and an abusive mother. The happiest years of her childhood, she recalls, were the three years she spent in a Gainesville, Texas, reform school. In her teens, she was subjected to repeated incidences of statutory rape by a male relative. At sixteen, she married a man who often beat her, even while she was pregnant. The marriage didn't last long.

"I am a rough woman," she later said of herself, "born into pain and anger and raised mostly by myself." To escape the pain of life, inflicted on her by an abusive mother and a succession of abusive men, she turned to alcohol, drugs, and lesbian relationships. She worked as a waitress, a barmaid, and as a shill for a traveling circus freak show. Pregnant twice before the age of twenty, she relinquished custody of her first child to her abusive mother and gave the second child up for adoption.

At age twenty-one, she became pregnant for a third time. That's when she met Sarah Weddington and Linda Coffee, a pair of young, ardent feminist lawyers from Texas. Norma McCorvey told Weddington her pregnancy was the result of rape (it wasn't) and that she wanted to know how to get an illegal abortion. Instead of helping Norma McCorvey get the abortion, the attorney had her sign a one-page legal affidavit. Weddington decided to turn Norma McCorvey's personal crisis into a legal test case to overturn Texas law prohibiting abortion.

"I wanted an abortion," Norma McCorvey recalled years afterward, "but Sarah Weddington and Linda Coffee, my lawyers, wanted to change the world. And they did. Sarah knew where I could get an abortion—she'd had one herself—but I was no use to her if I wasn't pregnant, so she didn't tell me. She actually dissuaded me from getting it done in Mexico. She didn't tell me it was a class-action suit on behalf of all American women, and she didn't tell me it would take so long. By the time she'd made herself and me famous, my daughter was already two years old and adopted."[2]

Norma's case went all the way to the Supreme Court—and the court shocked the sensibilities of the entire nation by completely overturning every restriction on abortion in all fifty states. Afterward, Norma McCorvey felt used and exploited by the prochoice feminist movement. "As far as my feminist lawyers were concerned back in the 1970s, I was just a dumb nobody," she recalls. "To these elite liberals who talk of tolerance, I was barely tolerable trash. If they hadn't found me to pin their politics on, they'd have found someone else to take advantage of."[3]

In the early 1980s Norma McCorvey went to work at abortion clinics, making six dollars an hour booking appointments. Her job, she says, included "persuading girls to come, lying to them that they weren't killing their babies, just bringing on a missed period. But I saw the cut up bodies in overflowing jars in the freezer, and I saw women changed forever.

Like so many other women working in the abortion mills, I thought I was doing good. So how come we felt our souls wilting? We never smiled and some of us turned to booze and drugs to dull our pain."⁴

Despite the fact that she believed in a woman's right to abortion, Norma McCorvey experienced acute mental anguish every year in January, when the anniversary of the *Roe v. Wade* decision came around. "I normally spent the latter part of November until around the first of February drunk and stoned," she told the Reuters news agency. "I did that roughly for about fourteen years."⁵ She was troubled by the things she saw at the clinic, such as a freezer packed with aborted babies. One day, while passing a playground with empty swings, the thought hit her: *Oh, no! The playgrounds are empty because there are no children! They've all been aborted!*

By the early 1990s disillusionment and disgust began to set in. "I started talking to the women before they would go in for their abortions, and after they would come out," she recalls. "It was the same thing over and over—they all regretted it.

"I was sitting there one morning and this lady walked in and she was in maternity clothes. And I said, 'The ob-gyn clinic is down the hall. This is where we do abortions.'

"And she said, no, that in fact this is what she wanted to do. And I said, 'But you're showing . . . And she said no, that she 'came to kill her baby'—word for word—and it shocked me. I had seen women come into the clinic but none of them had been wearing maternity clothes. They were just wearing regular clothes. And I had a real problem with that. I left, I took off work for two weeks. I started drinking again. And I had been clean, sober since 1989."⁶

In 1995 the pro-life organization Operation Rescue set up an office next door to the Dallas abortion clinic where Norma worked. "We were neighbors for a year," she recalls. "I'm sure God set it up. There we abortionists were, supposedly on the side of human enlightenment, calling the Christians 'terrorists,' cussing them, spitting on them and phoning the cops and press to beat them up on the sidewalk and in the newspapers. The 'terrorists' took it. They never turned violent. They prayed for us."

During that year, a girl named Emily, the daughter of one of the Operation Rescue workers, befriended Norma McCorvey. Emily told Norma that her own mother had nearly aborted her—but, thank God, she made a different choice just in time. As Norma told a correspondent for the *London Daily Telegraph*, "It was Emily who made me see that all those 35 million dead babies were real people too. They were individuals just like me, except most of them might have been better people.

"It was Emily and the Christians who showed me how hollow and poisoned my life had been. They led me to Jesus. And when I was baptized in a Dallas swimming pool in 1995, I smiled for the first time in years. I smiled harder than I ever remembered. The self-loathing had stopped. And I wasn't helping kill babies anymore.

"The pro-aborts, as I call them, had never liked or trusted me. I wasn't one of them either in terms of class or conviction. When I went over to the 'enemy,' they got really nasty."[7]

Pro-abortion feminists were understandably embarrassed when "Jane Roe" of *Roe v. Wade* jumped to the pro-life side. They tried to talk their way around the reality of Norma McCorvey's profound change of heart by making a contrived distinction between "Jane Roe" and Norma McCorvey. Feminist columnist Ellen Goodman wrote, "In the end, this was not the conversion of Jane Roe. It was the seduction of Norma McCorvey."[8] And Rheta Grimsley Johnson tried to dismiss

Norma McCorvey's conversion with an acid put-down: "Jane Roe is in the history books. Norma McCorvey we'll remember for at least fifteen minutes."[9]

The truth is that Norma McCorvey—her soul, her spiritual rebirth, and her moral transformation—is truly eternal. It is "Jane Roe" who has ceased to exist. "Jane Roe" is a legal fiction. But God is truly alive in the heart and life of a living, breathing woman named Norma McCorvey. She was not "seduced" by "anti-choice fundamentalists," as Ellen Goodman would like to believe. She was—to quote the title of Norma McCorvey's recent autobiography—*Won by Love* (Thomas Nelson, 1998). She was won by the Christlike love of genuine pro-life Christians and by the forgiving, transforming love of God Himself.

Innocent Blood on Our Hands

If "Jane Roe" herself, the woman whose case launched thirty-five million abortions, can experience peace, a new birth, and a new life in Christ, then any woman who has been through the experience of abortion can turn to Jesus Christ and find forgiveness, peace, and salvation.

The taking of an innocent life is a great sin. But the love of God is greater than even our greatest sins. God has made it possible for you and me and Norma McCorvey and every other sinner to be delivered and forgiven of anything we have ever done. He has made it possible for us to be transformed, so that our lives are turned in a completely new and righteous direction.

Becky Pippert, an author with InterVarsity Christian Fellowship, had a friend, a young woman we'll call Sally, whom she had helped lead to Christ. After Sally committed her life to Christ, she began to experience unbearable guilt over an abortion she underwent some years earlier. So she went to Becky and told her how troubled she was. "Becky, I've taken an innocent life," she said. "I've killed my baby. How can God ever forgive me after what I've done?"

"You've asked God to forgive your sin and remove all your guilt," Becky replied. "You've asked Jesus to be your Lord and Savior. He has done that."

"I can't believe that. Not after what I've done. God could never forgive me for killing my baby."

Becky silently prayed for the right words to say to this young woman, and then she began to speak. "Sally," she said, "you may think of yourself as a murderer—and you are exactly right. But you know what? You were a murderer long before you ever had that abortion, and so am I. You and I both have innocent blood on our hands."

"What do you mean? Whose innocent blood?"

"Jesus'. You and I nailed Jesus Christ to the cross and killed Him. Our sin caused God the Father to send Jesus to die for us."

"I never thought of it that way."

"Sally, do you think God has forgiven you for that?"

She hesitated. "Well," she said at last, "yes, I believe God has forgiven me for that—but I just can't believe He can forgive me for the abortion."

"Sally," Becky replied, "God has forgiven you and me for killing His own Son, Jesus. That is the worst crime anyone could ever commit. If God can forgive us for killing His own Son, won't He also forgive you for the abortion?"

And when that realization finally broke through on Sally's heart, she was free and at peace with herself and God.

"Deliver me from the guilt of bloodshed, O God, / The God of my salvation," wrote David the Psalmist, who was once guilty of taking an innocent life, "And my tongue shall sing aloud of

Your righteousness . . . As far as the east is from the west, / So far has He removed our transgressions from us."[10]

And the apostle Paul, who had been a persecutor of innocent Christian men, women, and children, said, "But God demonstrates His own love toward us, in that while we were still sinners, Christ died for us . . . For the wages of sin is death, but the gift of God is eternal life in Christ Jesus our Lord."[11] We all have innocent blood on our hands—but God's love and forgiveness are deeper than our deepest sin.

AIDS: Curse or Wake-Up Call?

I was shocked when I heard of the murder of Gianni Versace. The famous Italian fashion designer was a nice, caring man who was also enormously talented and creative. But in July 1997 a crazed gunman on a killing spree shot Versace at his oceanside Miami mansion. I did a number of his runway shows, as well as a series of Versace ads during the early 1980s that were shot by the brilliant photographer, Avedon. I appeared in the ads along with Brooke Shields, Rene Russo, Kelly LeBrock, Gia, and other models. During the photo sessions, Versace would often come to the sets and watch the creative process.

In March 1981 during one of those Versace ad shoots, a group of us were staying in a hotel in Italy. Around five in the morning, I was awakened by shouts of "*Fuoco! Fuoco!* Fire! Fire!" People were running through the halls, banging on doors, waking everybody up and yelling at us to get out of the hotel.

I jumped out of bed, and my first thought was the advice my mother gave me: "If you're ever in a fire, don't take time to get dressed. Don't take your purse or any belongings. Just run out of the building and save your life."

So what did I do? I defied my mother's advice! I got dressed and I took my purse with me. I *did* remember to take the stairs, not the elevator.

I got downstairs and our whole group was gathered out-side—all except Suga, our Japanese hairdresser. I knew what room Suga was in because every night he rolled my hair in pink rollers before I went to sleep (the models in the Versace ads had very curly hair). When I saw that Suga wasn't with the rest of us, I told one of the male models what room he was in and sent him upstairs to get him.

We saved Suga's life that night. Unfortunately, he only lived a few more years before dying of AIDS. Suga was gay, and so was Gianni Versace. It's no secret, of course, that the fashion community is very much a gay community. Understandably, in my career I became acquainted with quite a number of homo-sexual men, and most of them were very nice people. They didn't go out of their way to put their lifestyle on public view. They were private people, not activists.

When I began modeling in New York in 1978, I was aware that if you had sex outside of marriage, you could get a venereal disease. The thought that you could get syphilis or gonorrhea—well, that was scary enough for me! But when people actually began dying of AIDS because of their sexual behavior, it was terrifying.

In 1979, a year after I came to New York, a man I knew died of AIDS—the first of many friends and acquaintances of mine who would eventually die of that disease. At the time, all of us in the fashion and modeling world thought this man simply died of an extremely virulent form of pneumonia. But as the AIDS plague became better understood, we all realized that, ultimately, he died of a sexually transmitted disease.

There are some who think that AIDS is God's "curse" on gay

behavior. If that is so, then other sexually transmitted diseases must be God's curse on heterosexual behavior. And liver disease must be God's curse on alcohol abuse. And obesity, heart disease, and diabetes must be God's curses on the sin of gluttony. And if AIDS is God's curse on gay behavior, who is God punishing when children get AIDS?

I don't believe AIDS is a curse. But I do think AIDS is a wake-up call and a warning. God has given us His moral laws, not to hurt us but to protect us against harm. If we ignore His moral laws, we do so at our own peril. Instead of being angry with God because there are natural consequences to sin, we should be grateful because He loved us enough to give us moral laws that show us how to live holy, healthy lives.

As a Christian, I don't have the option of forming my opinions out of thin air. I have to base my beliefs on what the Bible says—and the Bible tells me that all sex outside of marriage is sin. Whether heterosexual or homosexual, sex outside of marriage violates God's law and brings harmful consequences to those who practice it.

So I have to conclude that homosexual behavior is sin. But at the same time, the man who cheats on his wife, or visits a prostitute, or engages in phone sex or cybersex is no less a sinner than the one who engages in homosexual behavior. The same is true of the woman who commits adultery or sells herself on the street. We are *all* sinners, and one class of sinner has no right to feel smug or superior to any other class of sinner. I have enough sins of my own—I don't need to go around condemning other people for theirs.

I have a problem, however, with that portion of the gay community (and it is only a portion) that wants to be declared a protected minority with special rights under affirmative action, such as hiring quotas. I have a problem with the idea of legislating "gay marriages," which would diminish and debase the sacrament of marriage God established as the foundation of the family. I don't believe in gay rights or black rights or any other group rights. I believe in *human* rights. All human beings, including gays, are created equal and should be treated equally, fairly, and with respect.

Having said this, I know that there are people who would call me a "homophobe." Well, *phobe* comes from *phobia,* which means "fear." The extreme gay fringe has tried to frame the discussion in such a way that all people who disagree with them are "homophobic," or *afraid* of homosexual people. Clearly, I'm not afraid of gay people—most of the gays I've known (and I've known many) are very nice, kind people. So if there's one thing I'm not, it's a homophobe.

When I hire someone or work with someone, I don't ask her about her sex life—it's none of my business. I would simply prefer that a private matter, such as a person's sexual behavior, would remain just that: private. I believe a lot of harm is caused, particularly to our children, when people wear their sexual behavior as a badge of identification.

I think it's a terrible thing that children these days have lost so much of the innocence of childhood, and have all sorts of sordid and inappropriate sexual information shoved in their faces. My nine-year-old son knows that the word *gay* refers to boys having boyfriends in a romantic sense, and even my four-year-old son has told me, "Boys don't kiss boys—that's wrong." I never told them this—they picked it up from the media or from friends.

One of the tragedies that results from so much media attention to the gay cause is that it leads many boys to feel self-conscious about having healthy, nonsexual friendships with other boys. At this stage of life, kids should not be thinking about the world in a sexualized way. They should be thinking about playing soccer and trading baseball cards and playing with their pals at school. They should not have information about sex (homosexual or heterosexual) thrust in their faces every time they turn around. I didn't have to deal with such issues when I was their age, and I wish the world would let my kids grow up in the same clean, moral climate I grew up in.

The Fragile Gift of Life

On one occasion in the early 1980s, I was about to be photographed for a Revlon ad, and my makeup was being applied by one of the top artists in the business. He had just started working on my face when someone took him aside and gave him the news that his boyfriend-lover had just died of AIDS.

In those days, before the development of AZT and other treatments for AIDS, a lot of HIV-infected people were trying to beat the disease with macrobiotic diets. They thought that if they consumed organically grown whole grains, beans, vegetables, dandelion root tea, and sea vegetables such as nori and wakame, they could stave off the AIDS virus. Of course, none of those remedies helped.

The makeup artist took the news of his lover's death without much visible emotion, and he went right back to work on my makeup. But as he kept working, I could feel the tension, the grief, and the fear he felt. I could feel it in his touch. You can tell a lot about a person's emotional state when he puts his hands to your face. This man wanted to be very professional and finish the job without breaking down, but I could tell he was dying inside.

He didn't talk about it—not directly. But at one point he

said very softly—either speaking to me or simply breathing a prayer—"Just help me get through this."

Sometime later, the makeup artist also died of AIDS.

I know that God truly loved that man. He loves all sinners, including you and me and gay men with AIDS. When Jesus walked the earth, He reached out in love and compassion to lepers and prostitutes and adulterers—those who were considered outcasts in their own society. If Jesus were walking the earth right now, I believe He would visit the AIDS ward, He would tell love-starved people that there is a God who loves them and is ready to receive them and forgive them. I pray that God points us to a cure for this terrible, wasteful disease, as well as other ravaging diseases such as cancer, multiple sclerosis, and Alzheimer's disease.

God loves homosexuals more than they will ever be loved by the AIDS Coalition to Unleash Power (ACTUP) or the Gay and Lesbian Alliance Against Defamation (GLAAD). God loves unwed mothers more than they will ever be loved by the National Organization for Women or Planned Parenthood or the National Abortion Rights Action League. God loves all of us more completely than we love ourselves, in spite of our deepest sins. He cares about our mortal, physical life—and He has made it possible for us to experience eternal life.

The life we live between birth and death, for however many years God may give us, is a fragile gift. And eternal life through Jesus Christ is an imperishable gift. Let's not waste any of it. Let's cherish life in all its forms. Let's protect and defend this gift God has given us—the precious and irreplaceable gift of life.

11
Defending Truth in a World of Lies

The most fascinating assignments I had as a model were the six swimsuit issues I did for *Sports Illustrated*. For the February 1982 issue, they sent me to Kenya, in eastern Africa, where I was photographed in a leather two-piece swimsuit while scores of spear-wielding Masai tribesmen danced, howled, leaped, and chanted behind me.

It was in October 1981, and there were several other people with me on the trip—an *SI* editor named Julie; the photographer; and a couple of assistants. I also met a man on that trip who later became my first husband. There was a teenage Kenyan boy with the crew who understood both English and Masai, and he translated for us.

I remember posing, trying to keep a smile on my face, trying to do what the photographer told me to do while this dancing, chanting, tribal frenzy was going on behind me. The noise behind kept getting louder and wilder, and the crew kept saying, "Don't turn around! Don't look behind you!" Well, *that* made me feel real secure! As the chanting got louder and closer, I got more and more anxious. The sun was going down, and the crew kept telling me, "We only have a little more light! Just stay with it, Kim! Stay with it!"

Though it was scary, it was also exciting. I could feel all this emotional energy coming from the Masai tribesmen behind me, and I knew that the camera would pick up that energy and create a fabulous set of shots. But in the next instant, I felt one of them come up behind me and lift up my hair. I guess my eyes got real big, and I asked in a panicky voice, "Ohmigosh, what are they doing now?!"

The young Kenyan interpreter said, "Don't worry. They think you are a blind goddess."

"A *what?!*"

"They think you are a goddess and you can't see. They've never seen blonde hair like yours before, so they think it is the hair of a goddess. And your eyes are blue, so they think you are blind."

We got the shots before the sun went down, and it made a great layout. It was one of the most intense cross-cultural experiences I've ever had. It was fascinating to see these Masai tribespeople looking into the side mirror of the Jeep, seeing themselves for the first time. My *Sports Illustrated* assignments took me to many exotic places, such as Thailand, Jamaica, and the Australian outback. I enjoyed the opportunity to sample different cultures.

But there was also a downside to my *SI* adventures.

"It's Art!"

There were always battles over outfits and coverage and cleavage, and I continually had to make it clear to Julie and the photographers what I felt comfortable doing and what I didn't.

Julie was very nice, very cordial—but she always held it over me and the other models that if we were a little more daring, if we bared a little more flesh—"This could be the cover!" Well, dangling a cover shot to a model is like dangling a bottle of Evian before a thirsty man in the desert!

We worked from sunup till sundown, with a break for an afternoon snooze when the sun got hot and high overhead (a high sun creates deep shadows under your eyes, so you look better when the sun is lower). Photographers love sunrises, so I would get up at 4:30 in the morning and put on my makeup in the dark. Shooting the *Sports Illustrated* swimsuit issues was some of the hardest work I ever did (the only thing harder is modeling furs outdoors in the summertime!).

People think the life of a model is a piece of cake: You stand there and look pretty and let them take your picture—what's so difficult about that? But it really is a lot of hard work, and I would always end up exhausted.

When the sunlight was fading, I would feel beat into the ground. But the photographer would say, "Just one more roll!" And he'd shoot another roll, and I'd think, *Finally!* And he'd say, "We still have some light—just one more roll!" It always seemed unbearable at the time, but months later, when I'd see the pictures in print, I'd think, "Hey! It was worth it!" Sometimes the best shots would come at the end of the shoot, when I was ready to quit.

The *Sports Illustrated* photographers love to position you on rocks or on a pebble-strewn beach, then contort you into some impossible position—then they say, "Oh, that's it! Hold it! Gorgeous!" Meanwhile, you've got little sharp stones digging into your hips, a palm frond tickling your shoulder, a cramp in your foot, and a crick in your neck—but you don't dare move a muscle or you'll spoil the shot!

But the worst part of this business is that you are constantly being asked to compromise your moral standards, your sense of what is right and wrong. There are pictures I look back on today and think, *Oh, why did I let them talk me into that?* And I can't simply blame it on the fact that I wasn't a born-again Christian at the time. I was raised with moral standards, I was raised to know right from wrong. I made choices, and some of them were poor choices.

I would sometimes find myself in situations where I would be right on the verge of uncomfortable with a certain pose or a certain outfit. And it was a lot like the old cliché of having an angel on one shoulder and a devil on the other. And the devil would say to me, "Oh, Kim! Don't you look great?! This will make a beautiful shot! This will be a cover for sure!" Then the angel would speak up: "Oh, Kim! Would your mother want you to do that?! Is that how you were raised?" But the devil would come back with, "Come on! Get over it! Grow up! This is a perfectly fine picture! *It's art!*"

That's the universal cop-out: "It's *art!* I don't have to maintain moral standards. I'm creating *art!*" Or so I sometimes told myself. There were some situations, some outfits, some poses that were just wrong, and I said "Absolutely, positively no!" There were others that were borderline, and I wasn't sure what to do. But most of the time, they would simply shoot so many pictures in such rapid succession, I wasn't sure what impression I was creating or which shots they would choose. I certainly had no control over anything that happened after the shutter clicked.

On one occasion they had me in a very flimsy yellow swimsuit, which wasn't too revealing as long as it was dry. But they didn't want to shoot it dry. They wanted everything wet, even my hair. I protested, but I ended up going in the water, and when I came out, the swimsuit ended up being a see-through. I was horrified. I didn't want my picture taken like that. "I'm really uncomfortable with this," I said. So they told me, "Don't worry, Kim—we'll retouch it later."

And I believed them! Of course, they didn't retouch it— why would they? The see-through look was *exactly* what they wanted! To this day, that photo still comes back to haunt me, and though I don't have many regrets from my modeling career, that shot is a *big regret*. If you send me any photo to autograph, I'll be happy to sign it for you—*but not that one!*

In time, I learned that if I was going to have any control over the statement I made with my own likeness, I had to think carefully in advance regarding the standards I would set for myself. I had to decide in advance that I was not going to be seduced by the "It's art!" rationalization. I had to decide in advance what was more important—"art" or truth.

A Fool for the Lord

Today, as a Christian and a mother, I want everything *in* my life and *about* my life to stand for the *truth* of my life. I want everything I do to reflect the truth that God is active in the world, that Jesus Christ is alive in my life, that the most important values in my life are faith, family, and moral virtue. Anything that would detract from these truths—even "art"—must be removed from my life.

In the Bible, truth is everything. Jesus Himself came into the world claiming to be the truth. "I am the way, the truth, and the life," He said. "No one comes to the Father except through Me."[1] And to those people who believed in Him, He said, "If you abide in My word, you are My disciples indeed.

And you shall know the truth, and the truth shall make you free."[2] I want to be on the side of truth, the side of Jesus Christ. I want my life and my daily actions to reflect His truth, because He has said, "He who does the truth comes to the light, that his deeds may be clearly seen, that they have been done in God."[3]

Usually, when I go on TV or make a personal appearance, I do so because I want to demonstrate the truth of Jesus Christ. That doesn't mean I will necessarily preach to people—but I want the light and truth of my values, my faith, and my life to shine through. I want my deeds as a follower of Jesus Christ to be clearly seen, that they have been done in God. Sometimes, trying to demonstrate the truth of Jesus Christ before the world can take me into some very strange places—

Like the tabloid talk show, *Geraldo.*

Some of my friends warned me not to go on Geraldo Rivera's show, but Geraldo led me to believe it would be a show on positive parenting and would be a good place to showcase my Christian, family-oriented values. At the time, I was hosting a show called *Healthy Kids* on the Family Channel. All along, right up to airtime, I was assured that it would be a show about raising healthy children.

But shortly before the show was to begin, I was informed that my co-panelists on the show were Lindsay Wagner, who was there to talk about her New Age ideas about health and nutrition, and Catherine Oxenberg, who had come with her guru, Dr. Something-or-other, to talk about chanting mantras and becoming one with the universe. As the show began, it became clear that the entire focus was on meditation and occultism and Eastern spirituality.

I thought, *Why am I here? This isn't what they told me at all! I never should have gotten into this!* I was way out of my comfort zone, and I just wanted to run. I was fuming inside: *Lord, just get me out of here!* But in the next few moments, I felt God saying to me, "Kim, here's an opportunity for you to speak My truth. You're here for a reason. So go ahead and speak."

I thought, *But what am I supposed to say with all this New Age weirdness going on?*

Just at that moment, Geraldo turned to me and said, "What is it, Kim? It doesn't look like you agree with what the others are saying."

And, of course, that was why I was there. Geraldo knew I was a Christian, and the only reason he wanted me on the show was to bait me and to provide some combustion for a hot discussion. (Geraldo, of course, is the guy who showed Jerry Springer how it's done.)

Well, the camera was on me, the microphone was in my face, the show was live from coast to coast—and it was time to put up or shut up. "That's right," I said. "I don't agree. I'm a Christian. As a Christian, you don't chant a mantra or get in touch with spirit guides or any of those things. As a Christian, you pray, you talk to God, the Creator of the universe."

The guru said, "Well, I pray to God too. And when I pray, I become one with the universe—and, therefore I am God!"

That got some applause from the people who thought they were Shirley MacLaine in another life. But I looked at him and said, "You are not God! Did you make the heavens and the earth? Can you create life out of nothing? Look, you are not God, I am not God; we're just dust that lives and breathes and walks around. God is so much more than you or I could ever be."

Well, Geraldo was ecstatic! He had gotten his controversy, just as he had planned. He starting running around the stage and out into the audience with his microphone, asking, "What do you think about what Kim just said?"

There was a time, a few years ago, when what I said wouldn't have been the least bit controversial. But today, faith in the God of the Bible is a minority position. Weirdness rules. As the Bible says,

> For since the creation of the world His invisible attributes are clearly seen, being understood by the things that are made, even His eternal power and Godhead, so that they are without excuse, because, although they knew God, they did not glorify Him as God, nor were thankful, but became futile in their thoughts, and their foolish hearts were darkened. Professing to be wise, they became fools.[4]

Almost the entire audience was against me. "I think it's fine to chant your mantra! What's wrong with that?" said one woman. "Why do you have to pray to a deity in the sky?" said another. "Why not just sit silently by yourself and connect with the universe?" And another made some shot about "narrow-minded" Christians. The show ended with people on the stage and in the audience meditating, their eyes closed, humming their mantras, their souls supposedly joined with the universe.

And me? I just sat on the stage with my eyes open, my arms folded, wondering why I get myself into these situations. I came out of the studio thinking, *I should have said this, I should have said that.* I found Ron and asked, "You saw it? What did you think? How did I do?"

Ron said, "You told the truth. You did fine."

Well, I suppose so. I didn't know what I was doing there— but I know that God always knows what He's doing. There's a part of me that wants to go into situations like that and always come out on top, always come out looking good, always come out feeling I did a great job and I was in complete control. I didn't feel that way on *Geraldo*. But that's okay. I've learned that whenever I'm in a situation like that, I just have to trust God and pray, "Lord, let Your will be done, not mine. Whatever You want to come out of my mouth, let it come out of my mouth. If You want me to be a fool, then I'll be a fool for You. Your obedient servant, Kim."

Feelings Versus Truth

Our culture has made an idol out of feelings. We now worship at the altar of emotion. People used to enter into marriage based on a vow, a solemn and binding commitment—but today people divorce and rip their homes apart for such flimsy, selfish reasons as, "I don't feel excited about this relationship—the feelings just aren't there anymore." We used to elect the president with the better plan, the better grasp of the issues, the better character; today we elect the president who's the best-looking or the best manipulator of our emotions, the one who "feels our pain."

People say, "If it feels good, do it. If it feels bad, it must be wrong." But that's a lie. A lot of things that "feel good" are harmful, even deadly. And a lot of things that "feel bad" are good for us. It hurts to have surgery—but surgery can restore our health and save our lives. Exercise can make you sore for a while—but it makes you healthy in the long run. Good medicine often tastes bad, but it helps you get better. Many things that feel bad are very good, and many things that feel good will hurt or kill you.

In *Star Wars,* Obi-Wan Kenobi told his young protégé,

"Trust your feelings, Luke!" But life is not a movie, and the Bible tells us not to trust our feelings alone. We are to obey the *truth*. "There is a way that seems right to a man," says Proverbs 16:25, "But its end is the way of death" (NKJV).

In order to obey the truth, I constantly find myself having to do things that feel bad. It feels bad to take a stand in a place of conflict. It feels bad to say what I believe on a show like *Geraldo* or *Politically Incorrect,* knowing that people are going to belittle my beliefs and call me "narrow-minded" or a "prude." But I have to do it; I have to obey the truth.

I don't enjoy disciplining my children when they do something they shouldn't. I'd rather do the things that make my kids happy, because I feel glad when they are happy. But in order to obey the truth of God's Word and my own God-given instincts as a mother, I discipline my children for their own long-term benefit and growth. If you love your children, it always feels bad to discipline them—but it's the right thing to do.

Feelings have their place, and we need to take them into account. Sometimes, I get a feeling in my stomach that a situation is just not right, even when logically it seems to be okay. I take such feelings into account when I make important decisions. But it's dangerous to give feelings more weight than they deserve. And it can be deadly to allow your life—or your society—to be run on the basis of feelings alone.

Today, we live in the time that was predicted long ago by the apostle Paul, who wrote, "For the time will come when [people] will not endure sound doctrine, but according to their own desires [that is, their feelings!], because they have itching ears, they will heap up for themselves teachers; and they will turn their ears away from the truth, and be turned aside to fables."[5] Today, people hear what they want to hear, they tune in the teachers, gurus, and leaders who make them feel good—and that is why our society has turned to fables and away from God's truth.

As a society, and particularly as Christians, we need to focus less on feelings and more on truth. We need to focus less on doing what feels good and more on doing what is right. We need to proclaim what we know to be true, regardless of how we feel.

The tragedy of our age is that people have forgotten what truth really is—or they have decided there is no such thing as truth. Instead of truth, all we get today is information and opinion. Our ears are constantly assaulted by noise. Our minds are stimulated constantly. There is a constant flood of talk available on TV, on radio, on the Internet, in print, over our fax machines and cellular phones. I know what I'm talking about, because I have all of these electronic gadgets—I even wear a pager watch, so if you have my pager number, you can find me anywhere.

There's nothing wrong with all of these information-age contraptions—but it's important that we know the difference between information and truth. The fact is, the places where you tend to find the most information are where you find the least truth. The real truth doesn't come blaring at you from some electronic device. It comes to you out of the silence and stillness of time spent alone with God, talking to Him, listening to His Spirit, reading His Word. Truth usually comes accompanied by peace and rest—not by noise and "a word from our sponsor."

We are the best-informed generation in human history—and the least wise. Our world and our airwaves are filled with highly educated fools—extremely intelligent people who have no wisdom, who couldn't recognize truth if it walked right up and bit them. The Bible warns us against becoming the kind of people who are "always learning" yet "never able to come to the knowledge of the truth."[6] But isn't that exactly what we've become? We've become fat with knowledge and starved for truth.

And when I say "we," I really do include myself! I have thought about going back to the university, getting some impressive letters after my name, getting some degrees so I can be better accredited as a spokesperson on health and nutrition issues. But I've decided I don't really want to major in knowledge. I really sense God whispering in my ear, telling me, "Kim, I want you to major in wisdom so you can become a better ambassador for Me." So I've said, "Okay, Lord. I'll do what You say. Instead of majoring in knowledge, I'll major in truth—Your truth."

The "Sin" of Being Judgmental

One way truth and wisdom have been destroyed in our society is by selling an entire generation on the false notion that it is a "sin" to be judgmental. You hear it all the time these days: "I can't stand Christians—they're so judgmental!" Or, "Who's to say what's right or wrong?" Or, "Your thinking is too black-and-white—when you have become more tolerant, progressive, and open-minded like me, you'll see that there are many shades of gray." (I *hate* the color gray!)

And the result of such thinking is all around us. Instead of values, we now have personal preferences. Instead of moral standards, we now have moral relativism. Instead of healthy families, we now have shattered families.

It's easy to see why so many people prefer to live in a "non-judgmental" world. "Look at me," they say. "I'm progressive, I'm a freethinker, I'm tolerant and broad-minded. See this little looped ribbon of tolerance I wear on my lapel? I would never lay judgment on another person (unless, of course, that person votes conservative or opposes abortion or smokes or is otherwise politically incorrect)." The "nonjudgmentalists" can go through life proud of their own tolerance, never having to antagonize anyone, never having to take a courageous moral stand, never having to do anything difficult or uncomfortable because of a "rigid" moral code or a set of religious values.

But there is a problem with that kind of thinking: It produces a world of moral and ethical chaos. Once we throw out values, morality, absolutes, and standards, once we deny ourselves the right to judge what is black and white, wrong and right in the world—we open the floodgates of hell.

Professor Robert Simon, who teaches at Hamilton College in New York state, made this discovery after twenty years of teaching philosophy. He says that today's generation of young people is different from previous generations because they have been brainwashed into the belief that there are no absolutes, no black-and-white truths. To some people, that may not seem like such a big deal when it comes to issues of lying, stealing, cheating on a test, or sex outside of marriage—issues our culture winks at.

But Professor Simon is disturbed that increasing numbers of students cannot bring themselves to acknowledge that the Holocaust was morally wrong! He sees increasing numbers of students who will not condemn as immoral the deliberate murder of millions of Jews by the Nazis during World War II—because that would be judgmental! They acknowledge that the Holocaust took place, and they personally find mass murder to be disagreeable—but Simon says that as many as 20 percent of his students express their disapproval only as a "personal preference," not a moral judgment. He quotes one of his students as saying, "Of course I dislike the Nazis, but who is to say they are morally wrong?"[7]

So now mass slaughter becomes just another matter of individual choice. Like the choice of whether or not to abort your baby. Or the choice of whether or not to have fries with that burger. This is what an ethic of "nonjudgmentalism" has brought us to.

We have made *judgmental* the only dirty word in our society. We forget that, embedded in that word *judgmental,* is the word *judgment.* When it becomes a crime to be judgmental, then we have lost our judgment. We have lost our ability to reason and weigh issues. We can no longer say mass murder or abortion or divorce or sex outside of marriage or pornography is wrong.

And why stop there? Since we're being so wonderfully tolerant and open-minded, why stop anywhere? There is no right, no wrong, no judgmentalism, no intolerance. Pedophiles and child pornographers, we no longer judge you. Ethnic cleansing in Bosnia? What's wrong with that? And maybe we should rethink the Civil War. After all, those people who tried to abolish slavery were terribly judgmental and narrow-minded. Besides, owning other human beings is just another lifestyle choice! It may not be for you and me, but who are we to judge slave owners? And you know, we really shouldn't be so quick to judge people who are hunting down whales or clear-cutting the rain forests! And shouldn't we show a little more tolerance for murderers and rapists and drug dealers?

Where does it end?

I know this sounds terribly intolerant, but I think it's time we exercise some judgment. It's time we recognize that, just as the Bible has been telling us for thousands of years, some things really are black and white, some things really are wrong or right. There are times when being tolerant is a sin, when being judgmental is a virtue. We live in a world where there is good and there is evil, and if we tolerate evil, we are evil ourselves.

I have learned that I must approach every situation in my life with an awareness of the moral issues involved. I must carefully, consciously *judge* (there's that word again!) every choice I make, asking myself, "Is this of God? Is this what God wants me to do? By choosing this direction or that direction, am I living out and obeying God's truth—or am I giving in to self or Satan?" Because many of the choices we make in life really are that stark and that important.

I am very conscious of the role God has given me. I continually ask myself how He would want me to act in every situation. I weigh everything. I exercise judgment. If that makes me "judgmental" by the off-kilter standards of this world, then so be it. But I'd rather be thought weird and narrow-minded and judgmental by the people of this world than to face the Lord in the next world, ashamed that I was too cowardly to speak His truth.

Image Versus Truth

Okay, now let's talk about hemorrhoids and yeast infections. A lot of people ask me: "Kim, you've been on the cover of *Vogue* and the *Sports Illustrated* swimsuit issues. You have such a glamorous image! Why on earth are you now doing commercials for hemorrhoid and yeast infection products?"

The answer may surprise you. Here again, it all comes down to something called *truth*.

In 1994, around the time my youngest, Noah, was born, Ron and I were having financial problems. Believe it or not, hockey stars and supermodels can make bad investments and bad business decisions—especially if they entrust their business affairs to the wrong people. So that was the situation that confronted us when the people at Pfizer came to me and asked me to appear in commercials for their Hemorid hemorrhoidal cream.

I was mortified. I said to my husband, "Ron, I'm a glamour girl! I've done magazine covers and fashion shows. I've built my reputation in the beauty world. Why would I go and do a commercial for something like—hemorrhoidal cream?!"

"Number one," he said, "you'd be helping other people. Number two, even though you've been a glamour girl, you've never been superficial—you also have a honest, unpretentious side to you. Number three, we need the money."

Number three was the clincher. So, after checking out the company and the product, I agreed to do the Hemorid commercials. As it turned out, they were elegantly produced, and I was presented as an authority figure. It could have been demeaning and embarrassing, and they could have said, "You're being well paid, so take the money and quit complaining." Instead, it was a pleasant experience.

The Hemorid commercials led directly to my syndicated TV show, *Your Mind and Body*. When the producers saw I could talk about hemorrhoidal creams with class and dignity, they figured I could do just about anything!

I started taping *Your Mind and Body* in 1995, and Time-Warner syndicated the show in 120 markets. It was hard work, often entailing fourteen-hour or longer days. There was a time we put in an entire day just to shoot a five-minute segment in Palm Springs in the summer. By the end of my first season, I was exhausted.

After my first season with the show, Time-Warner was trying to decide whether or not they should commit to a second season. They went to the national convention where syndicated shows are sold to affiliate stations, and after the convention they made the decision to drop the show.

The vice president of the syndicated programming division at Time-Warner called me, and she was terribly apologetic. "Kim," she said, "I'm so sorry to have to tell you this, but I'm afraid we've decided not to renew the show." She continued talking for about ten minutes, telling me how much they appreciated my hard work, how they hoped they'd be able to find another project for me, on and on and on, trying to spare my feelings. One of the last things she said was, "You know, Kim, when God closes a door, He always opens a window."

Well, it was nice of her, but honestly! My feelings weren't hurt. I wasn't really bothered in the least. Jobs come and go in my business, and it's not the end of the world. Throughout the call, I kept trying to tell her, "It's all right, I'm okay, I really don't mind, you don't need to let me down easy, thanks for calling!" Finally, I got off the line, and got back to whatever I had been doing before she called.

Ten minutes later, the phone rang. It was my manager. "I've got this great commercial for you," he said.

"Okay. What's the product?"

"It's for Monistat, the yeast infection product."

"You're joking, right?"

"Actually, this is on the level."

My first thought was, *God, You don't really want me to do a commercial about yeast infections, do You? I already did this hemorrhoid thing! Now, yeast infections?!*

But as it turned out, God was telling me, "Yes, Kim, that's exactly what I want for you."

And my manager went on to explain what it would entail. I would be paid three times as much money for six days of work on the Monistat commercial as I was paid for forty days of work on *Your Mind and Body* for Time-Warner! That meant I would make a lot more money, yet have a lot more free time left over to spend with my children. And this offer arrived only ten minutes after I got the call telling me my syndicated show was canceled. It turned out that the Time-Warner vice president knew what she was talking about; God had closed a door and opened a great big window, all in the space of ten minutes.

Still, I had my doubts. I mean, yeast infections! I had already taken a bit of ribbing for the hemorrhoid cream commercials. For example, *Time* magazine led its coverage of the 1996 Republican National Convention by noting that the party had invited "swimsuit model and hemorrhoid cream spokeswoman Kim Alexis to address delegates on the importance of God and family."[8] I really wasn't sure that I wanted my résumé to read "hemorrhoid and yeast infection spokesperson."

I talked it over with Ron, and he said, "Kim, you've got to take the job."

"Ron," I said, "you don't understand. This is yeast infections. I've got these hemorrhoid cream commercials running—and now this. Look at me. I've done more glamour covers than any other model in history—over five hundred covers. *That's* the image people have of me—not hemorrhoids and yeast infections!"

"Oh," said Ron. "If it's your *image* you're concerned about—"

As usual, Ron had nailed it. He was right. One reason Ron and I are so good together is that he thinks one way, I think another, and when we put it all together it always comes out as God wants it to. Ron helped me to see that I was concerned about my *image* when I should have been concerned about the *truth*.

And what is the truth about Kim Alexis Duguay? That I'm some dazzling, lofty goddess of beauty who steps forth from the pages of *Vogue*? No way! Hey, it's just me, Kim from Lockport! I'm a practical mom. I've done poopy diapers, I've run marathons, I'm a human being like everybody else—so why not be honest about it?

I figured out that God had brought me to this place, that He had given me these opportunities, because He wanted to let me be more real, more personal, more transparent, open, and honest about who I truly am. So I said to God, "Okay, okay, I'll do it! I'll be real! I'll talk about external itching and intimate women's stuff—but, Lord, I've got to tell You, this is really not the kind of thing I thought You would put me in!"

As it turned out, however, the television commercials were done in a very elegant, tasteful way. Again, I was presented as an authority figure, and treated as a spokesperson people would respect and listen to. I got a lot of positive response from people about the Monistat commercials.

One of the funniest responses I got was from the thirteen-year-old neighbor boy who said, "I saw you on a TV commercial last night—what was that for again?"

The boy's mother was standing behind him, and she was horrified. "Get over here!" she said. "Don't ask her such things!"

I just laughed and told the boy, "Honey, don't worry about it. It's a girl thing."

Commercials for hemorrhoid creams and yeast infection products may not be very glamorous—but glamour isn't reality. Hemorrhoids and yeast infections are real problems, and people need to know how to solve those problems. That's the truth—and that's why you see me on TV talking about those problems.

These days I'm a lot less concerned with image and a lot more concerned with truth.

Taking a Stand for the Truth

I have an interesting vantage point, because I keep one foot in each world—the Christian world and the secular world. I do segments for *The 700 Club,* and we always pray before we begin taping. Everyone you meet at the Christian Broadcasting Network studios in Virginia Beach, where we do the show, is a believer, a brother or sister in Christ. There's a very warm, positive, godly atmosphere there.

But then the next day, I'm back out in the world, going to a secular studio, having lunch at a sandwich shop, hanging around people who don't have the same worldview and values that I do. In fact, I sometimes feel they speak a different language. I'm constantly surrounded by people who curse and blaspheme as a normal part of their everyday vocabulary. After being in the company of Christians for a while, it's a little jarring when someone swears or tells a dirty joke around me. It would be real easy to just let the cursing or the jokes go by, and sometimes I do.

But sometimes, I hear someone swear in my presence—"Oh, my God!" or "Jesus Christ!"—and I just very gently say, "Yes, He's alive! He's my Friend! Do you know Him too?" If I know the person is an atheist, I might even say, "I thought you didn't believe in Him."

The comeback is usually something like, "Oh, I don't believe in Him, but I can still use His name. After all, Jesus was just an ordinary man—not anyone special!"

"Well," I reply, "if He's just an ordinary man, if His name means nothing to you, why don't you just say, 'John Hancock!'? That name's just as ordinary to you, and then you won't offend anybody."

Sometimes that's all it takes to take a stand for the truth. But sometimes taking a stand can be a lot more costly.

Years ago, before I became a born-again Christian, I was offered a lot of money to appear in an ad for cigarettes. I refused the assignment, and the people at the modeling agency were understandably upset. After all, they were losing a big commission! "How can you turn down a job like that?" But I had to think of my own integrity. I fly on a lot of airplanes, so if I'm on a plane and the passenger next to me lights up, what right do I have to ask him to please not smoke? (This, of course, was in the days before smoking was banned on domestic flights.) He'd just hold up the magazine he's reading with my cigarette ad on the back cover, and he'd say, "Lady, if you can cash the check for that ad, then I can light up." And he'd be absolutely right.

After I came to Christ and became an ambassador for Him, of course, the stakes became much bigger than my own integrity—I had the Lord's reputation to uphold as well!

Shortly after Noah, my youngest, was born, I was approached by a company that sells a well-known weight loss product. They offered me a contract in the high six-figures to endorse their product. "You've had your baby, and you want to get back to your original weight," they said. "So just take our product, and we'll have a doctor keep track of your weight loss. Then we'll shoot a commercial in which you say, 'Look at all the weight I lost while taking this product!'"

There was just one problem: Ron and I are into organic vegetables, a lot of protein, and pure food. This diet product was made of sugar and chemicals, and I don't believe in drinking sugary chemicals to replace a meal. There were friends and relatives who told me, "Sign the contract! Drink the stuff! Take the money! Hey, for that kind of money, I'd promote canned antifreeze as a weight loss product!"

And don't think I wasn't tempted—that was a lot of money! But Ron and I discussed it, and we called Ty Thornton, our good friend who is a knowledgeable nutritionist, and we discussed it with him. In the end, there was only one decision to make: I had to turn it down. It wasn't really hard to say no, because I'm very clear on what my principles and values are. I also have a great trust in God's goodness, and I knew that if I said no to this opportunity, He would give me something else, something He really wanted me to do.

It was a costly decision but I never regretted it, because my image and my integrity and my ambassadorship for Christ are all bound together. I can't sacrifice one without tarnishing the other. Even though there's nothing immoral or unspiritual about that particular product, it would have been a violation of my Christian principles to endorse it. It would be falsehood— a betrayal of the truth—to talk about good nutrition one minute, and lend my support to this chemical guck the next.

I was once involved in a conversation over dinner with some friends, a man and a woman. Something happened in this casual conversation with friends that impressed me with the importance of maintaining a reputation for honesty, integrity, and truth. I don't remember the subject we were discussing, but I recall that I made a statement that the man found surprising, and he leaned over to the woman and asked, "Is Kim pulling my leg or is she telling the truth?"

"Oh, if Kim said it," she replied, "it's the truth. Kim doesn't ever lie."

Whoa! I thought. *That's a lot to live up to!*

But if I'm going to represent Jesus Christ, then I have to live my life and speak my message with integrity. I have to be a person whose word is reliable, who always speaks the truth. In a world where people commonly take the position that "you have your truth and I have my truth," we need to take a stand for *real* truth, *God's* truth—and we need to be people who can be trusted to always "speak the truth in love,"[10] no matter what it costs.

I was a spokesperson for a weight management product called CitriMax, a 100 percent natural, fat-inhibiting, appetite-suppressing product containing hydroxycitric acid, a pure extract from a particular Asian citrus fruit. It's for people who are trying to lose weight naturally. As part of my job promoting CitriMax, I did satellite media tours, in which I would sit in front of a video camera while I was linked by satellite to a number of TV stations around the country. There were interviewers at all these various remote sites, and while I couldn't see the interviewers, I could hear them through an earpiece. I'd talk to the camera and do a live interview with a lot of interviewers at once.

During the course of this satellite tour, one interviewer just went completely over the edge and became totally hostile. I had no warning that anything like this might happen. He actually led off his interview with, "How dare you! How can you go on the air and talk about a product that encourages women to be thin and anorexic? Here you are, coming straight out of the modeling profession, a business that promotes an unhealthy self-image for women, and now you're saying that women aren't good enough unless they are thin and anorexic like fashion models! Because of you, a lot of women are going to go out and self-induce vomiting or starve themselves!"

I have no idea what triggered this guy. Maybe he had gone through a lot of pain because of an anorexic daughter or a bulimic girlfriend. Or maybe he just imagined himself to be a

Mike Wallace–type hostile interrogator. Whatever his problem might have been, he took it all out on me.

Finally, I stopped him. "Hold it," I said. "I'm not encouraging anyone to become anorexic or bulimic. I just want people to be healthy, and that's why I'm here to talk about a product that is, number one, healthy, and number two, natural—no chemicals. Now, the fact is that a lot of people in this world are overweight, and it is also a fact that being overweight is unhealthy. I didn't make that up, it's a fact. God designed the human body to be optimally healthy at a certain weight. Some people may say it's okay to be big and beautiful, but the fact is that we were not designed to be big, we were designed to be healthy."

He responded, "But the entire modeling industry promotes a superthin stereotype—"

"I don't deny that," I said, "but I'm not here representing the modeling industry. I'm here representing a healthy, natural product. I'm not here to promote an image, I'm here to promote good health. Look, that superthin stereotype is not me. I'm a big girl, big-boned and muscular, and I've always been accused of being overweight, not a thin little wisp of a model. I'm here because I want to see normal people experience normal healthy lives, without consuming a lot of sugar and chemicals. So why is that a problem with you?" During the course of the interview, I was able to set him straight.

Before I met Ron, I wouldn't have been able to confront a media situation like that. A hostile interviewer could have shredded me on-camera, and I wouldn't have had any idea how to answer. But my husband has taught me so much about how to stand for the truth, even in a hostile or confrontational situation.

I've seen him in those kinds of situations, and when someone gets in his face, he handles it calmly but firmly. He doesn't respond with hostility or aggression of his own. He simply takes control of the situation. His way is to turn it around and say, "You've got a problem with me? Let me tell you what your problem really is." And he proceeds to correct the other person in a straightforward, no-nonsense way.

I've learned from that. I've discovered that when people challenge me or confront me, I don't have to shrink from the confrontation. I can simply take charge and respond with the truth. If, for example, someone is accusing me of promoting an unhealthy thin-model stereotype and I know I'm really trying to help people and improve their lives, I can simply state the truth.

I also did radio interviews for CitriMax—usually by phone with radio talk show hosts in various cities. I was surprised to find out how many obnoxious, egotistical Howard Stern wanna-bes there are doing local radio talk shows around the country. One interviewer began with this little grabber: "Hey, I'm fat! And I understand that you don't like fat people! So what are you trying to do—get everyone to be skinny like you? What's wrong with being fat?"

Another had a very original approach: "Kim, I think this would be a good time to let my audience in on my big secret: You used to date me."

"What?" Of course, I didn't know this guy from Adam.

"You dated me—and you wanted me."

"Uh—could we just get back to what I was brought on the air for?"

"Oh, yeah, I get it! You just want to sell your product, don't you?"

"I want to help people," I said, "and CitriMax has helped a lot of people."

Well, he continued with his shock-jock shtick for a few more seconds, and I decided I had heard enough. I told his listeners they should be ashamed to listen to such garbage, then I hung up and got on with my day. There was a time when people like that would get to me and spoil my mood for days. Not anymore. I don't let people roll over me or rattle me. When someone is wrong, I simply stand up and speak the truth.

I think God has been teaching me, toughening me, leading me through various experiences, and getting me to the point where I will take a stand for the truth—not just for a product, but for my faith and for important issues like defending the family, protecting life, and living morally pure lives. I've learned that God wants me to wade right in and deliver the message He's given to me.

When hostility comes, I get a sick feeling in my stomach—but I don't let that stop me. As Christians, we need to stand up to people who oppose God and His truth. We need to say, "You're wrong, and God's truth is right." One reason there is so much evil in the world today is that good people let bad people get away with lies and bad behavior. By our silence and timidity, we are accessories before and after the fact. It's time for good people to take a stand and speak the truth.

12

A Model for Action

I am not a political person. I frankly don't understand why we need to have political parties. People who know me know that I'm not a political activist by any means.

So a lot of people were surprised to see me standing on the platform at the 1996 Republican National Convention in San Diego. It's interesting how that came about, because I was actually added to the program at the last minute.

I had been scheduled to speak at a "SALT Shaker" rally at Mariner's Point in San Diego around the same time as the convention—August of 1996. SALT stands for "Savior's Alliance for Lifting the Truth," and it was a Christian young people's rally designed to send a message to the politicians at the convention that American youth care about such things as morality and sexual purity. When the Republican convention organizers heard that I would be appearing at the rally, they said, "What's this? Supermodel Kim Alexis is going to talk about values and virtue?" So they invited me to be a presenter at the convention, and I agreed.

If I had felt that the Democrats, the Libertarians, or even the Kiwanis Club offered the best opportunity to restore faith, family, and moral virtues to a rightful place in our society, that's whose convention I would have gone to, that's whose cause I would have supported. It just happened that, in 1996, I saw the Republican Party as the party of family and morality, the party that supported religious freedom and religious conscience—all the values that were most important to me. So I agreed to do my little bit for the cause by appearing at the Republican National Convention.

Security was very tight around the convention. They had people who looked under my limousine for bombs, and access to the convention hall was very tightly controlled. At the rehearsal, I was impressed with how efficient everything was. Every speaker, every video, all the lighting and music was carefully choreographed, rehearsed, timed, and polished to perfection. The convention people were very helpful, friendly, and professional.

I came back later that same evening to give my presentation at the convention. You could feel the tingle of electricity in the air. The convention is live TV, and when those lights and cameras come on, everything changes, everyone feels it. There is an emotional energy that makes everything and everyone glow with excitement. I could feel that excitement, a kind of thrill mingled with anxiety, and I dealt with the pressure by sitting in the green room with other people, talking and keeping my mind off what was going on in the convention hall. I ran into an old girlfriend from Florida in the green room—she was working for Bob Dole and the RNC, and I hadn't seen her in a long time, so it was a gift from God to be able to renew our acquaintance.

"Lord, This Is Your Situation . . ."

I don't get overly nervous in media situations, because I'm used to audiences and live TV. After three years on ABC's *Good Morning America,* I was accustomed to live television. I had long ago learned that if I know my script, I'm in control. Even if the TelePrompTers blow out, I can stay poised and confident, because I know what I'm supposed to do and what I'm supposed to say. So the edginess I felt was not fear, but an edge of energy—the kind that lights up my face and enables me to do my best before the cameras.

Let me give you an idea of how tightly controlled the schedule was: An Olympic wrestler was to speak at 5:50 P.M., I was to come on at exactly 5:55 P.M. to introduce some video clips, and then Dan Quayle was to follow me at precisely 6:04 P.M.— not 6:03, not 6:05, not sixish, but 6:04 on the dot. There were people with stopwatches timing everything to the hundredth of a second. The entire event was carefully designed to flow, one presentation building to the next, each segment going click, click, click with absolute precision.

But this, of course, was live TV—and anything can happen!

As the time for my presentation approached, I left the green room and waited in the wings for my turn on the stage. Standing around me were some very tense-looking guys with scripts and headsets—media people who called the shots and gulped Maalox tablets by the handful. The Olympic wrestler was onstage, comparing the election to the Olympics and talking about the other athletes who had turned in gold-medal performances in Atlanta—the women's basketball team, Michael Johnson, Kerri Strug—

But then something went wrong. The wrestler was supposed

to stop talking and make his exit—but he just kept on talking! And as he talked, he called two people to come onstage—two victims of the Centennial Park bombing in Atlanta, one of them in a wheelchair. I thought, *This didn't happen in the rehearsal!*

The guys with the scripts, headsets, and Maalox went ballistic. "Oh, no!" moaned one. "What's he doing out there?"

Another threw up his hands and groaned, "He's off-script! We're a minute over—and he's still going!"

That's where my *Good Morning America* experience counted. I knew I had to edit my remarks while I was on-camera. I knew I could do it, not a problem—but now there was an added edge of stress to the situation. Suddenly, I didn't feel I had everything under control. I began to experience an attack of the killer butterflies. Inwardly, I prayed, *Lord, this is Your situation—You handle it, okay?*

Finally, the wrestler and his two friends left the stage. So I went out and began my presentation. "Our nation," I said, "was built on a strong moral foundation, but many people feel we've been losing our moral compass, that we need to get back to basics. The basics include instilling in our children a clear sense of right and wrong, and taking responsibility for the choices we make and actions we take. The basics include working to make our families strong and close—"

At that point, the guys with headsets began frantically signaling me and whispering to me: "Cut! Stop! Introduce the video and make your exit!" So I condensed the rest of my talk into a single sentence: "I truly believe that a strong sense of family is what God wants for us." Then I intro'd the video clips.

Even though I didn't get to say everything I had come to say, my brief appearance at the Republican National Convention led to many other opportunities to speak out for God, family, and morality. As I've shared in this ongoing dialogue with people about family, faith, and values, I have felt a need to say all the things I didn't get to say that night in San Diego. Finally, in this book, I've had my say—no time constraints, no TelePrompTer, no anxious guys in headsets telling me to cut my message short.

My "Model for a Better Future"

I believe that if every person on the planet would follow the example and teachings of Jesus Christ, our world would become a better place than Shangri-la, Utopia, and Disneyland rolled into one! You may say, "But I'm not a Christian! You want everyone to think and believe exactly as you do! What about pluralism and religious freedom? You're being intolerant of my beliefs!"

No, I'm not. Jesus never demanded that people believe in Him, so I won't, either. I can't force Jesus on you, and I would never try. But you know what? *All* the world's great religions acknowledge that Jesus was—at the very least—a great moral and ethical teacher. Judaism, Islam, Buddhism, and Hinduism all hold Jesus in high regard as a model for our lives. So, even in a pluralistic society like America, even if you are not a Christian, Jesus can be a model for your values and your conduct.

What would a world modeled on His words and example be like? First of all, it would be a world of love, forgiveness, and harmony. In Mark 12:29–31, Jesus said, "The first of all the commandments is: 'Hear, O Israel, the LORD our God, the LORD is one. And you shall love the LORD your God with all your heart, with all your soul, with all your mind, and with all your strength.' This is the first commandment. And the second, like it, is this: 'You shall love your neighbor as yourself.' There is no other commandment greater than these" (NKJV). It was Jesus who formulated the golden rule, who taught us to love our enemies and forgive those who sin against us, who reached out and called the little children to Himself.

A world that is truly modeled on the life and words of Jesus would be a peaceful and gentle place; a place where human needs are met with mercy and compassion; a place where it's safe to be a child, and no child would ever be subject to abortion, abuse, neglect, molestation, domestic violence, child pornography, hunger, or poverty; a place where broken relationships are healed with unselfish love—love that is not an emotion, but a decision; a place where leaders and politicians would see themselves as servants, not masters and bosses; a place where good is exalted and evil is confronted; a place where there are no divorces, no broken homes, no kids suffering the loss of an intact family; a place where there is no more adultery, pornography, or other sexual sin and depravity; an orderly and law-abiding place. That's not just my model for a better future. That's God's model. That's what Jesus came to show us.

Why have we ignored and neglected this simple model for so long? What's wrong with us? Why have we allowed our society and our world to get into such a mess?

If we want to build a better future for ourselves and our children, it must begin with us—those of us who wear the label "Christian." I believe that one of the primary reasons our society is in such a mess today is that Christians are not following the example of Jesus. We certainly can't expect non-Christians to pay attention to the model of Jesus if we Christians ignore it ourselves.

Instead of making the Christian faith *appealing* to others, we have sometimes made it *appalling*. Instead of demonstrating Christian love, forgiveness, and unity, we have bickered and fought with one another in the Christian community. If we are going to make a better world and a better future, then we have to be better Christians. We have to pattern our lives after the One we claim to follow.

As God told His people thousands of years ago, "If My people who are called by My name will humble themselves, and pray and seek My face, and turn from their wicked ways, then I will hear from heaven, and will forgive their sin and heal their land."[1] Those words are as true today as when God first spoke them to Israel in the Old Testament. Renewal must begin with Christians, people who are called by Christ's own name. It begins with our humility, our prayers, and our repentance. If we will be faithful in these things, then God has promised to bring healing to our land.

I don't claim to be a perfect Christian. But I'm a sincere Christian. I make mistakes and I sin, but I really want to follow the Lord. If I ever get off-track, I've asked my husband, my pastor, and my Christian friends to hold me accountable and help me get back on the path. That's what the Christian life is all about—not being perfect, but being committed, honest, and accountable.

One of the ways I'm following Jesus these days is by joining my husband, Ron, in his Christian outreach through the ministry of hockey. No, that's not a misprint. I said the *ministry* of hockey! Ron works with Hockey Ministries International and Cross Ice Ministry—and I get to strap on skates, grab a stick, and hit slap shots with the big boys! Along with Ron and a number of other Christian hockey players, I get out on the ice and play exhibition hockey games. It's fun—and because we are Christians, no one spends too much time in the penalty box or loses very many teeth. These games raise money to help the homeless, and we have a chance to talk to people about our faith. Ron also coaches kids in hockey clinics, where he talks to them about character, faith, and values.

In everything I do—whether it is getting out on the ice with Ron, going on television or radio, stepping onto the platform at the Republican National Convention, or writing this book— my goal is to leave this world a little bit better than I found it. I want to leave some of the sweet fragrance of Jesus and His Spirit wherever I go. I want to attract people to the wonderful Friend I have found.

When Jesus began His church, He began with twelve close friends. They were fishermen and tax collectors—just ordinary working-class people, not celebrities or kings or scholars. Jesus' friends learned from His example and copied His life, then spread out and influenced others, reproducing the life of Christ in other lives—one life at a time. Today, the church of Jesus numbers in the millions. That was no accident. That was God's deliberate plan.

That's why Jesus said, "What is the kingdom of God like? And to what shall I compare it? It is like a mustard seed, which a man took and put in his garden; and it grew and became a large tree, and the birds of the air nested in its branches."[3] That's why the apostle Paul says, "But God has chosen the foolish things of the world to put to shame the wise, and God has chosen the weak things of the world to put to shame the things which are mighty."[4]

As I was completing work on this book, I received a letter that reminded me in a powerful way of how God uses weak things, foolish things, little mustard-seed things, to achieve His purposes in the world.

The letter was from a man in prison, and he was writing about an autographed picture of me he had received. When people request a picture, I always enclose a sheet of Scripture quotations along with the photo. It's a small thing I do as a witness to my faith in Christ—but as I found out when I received this letter, you never know what God can accomplish with the little things we do in His name. The letter from the man in prison (which has been edited slightly) read:

Mrs. Kim Alexis,

Hi. Today a friend of mine traded me an autographed photo of you. I pulled your photo out of the manila envelope to admire, and I recognized you from your Rapid White infomercial. I also noticed a green piece of paper in the envelope, and I pulled it out. The heading you wrote read "Scripture for You!" The second Scripture quotation had a profound effect on me.

Earlier this morning, I was walking to the chow hall, mulling in my mind the memory of a certain person and his actions. He stole a few thousand dollars from my room as I was taking a shower and ran away before I came out. A year has passed since then and during that time I have learned his full name, his girlfriend's name, his state and city, and whom he's staying with.

I was planning to murder this man. God knows I wanted to, in hopes my festering rage would be satisfied. The only reason I was in debate with this was my concern for my immortal soul. I want my life to be in line with God's plan, and I was trying to rationalize this man's death for what he put me through versus what the Bible says.

The answer came to me as I read your Bible quotations: "Beloved, do not avenge yourselves, but rather give place to wrath; for it is written, 'Vengeance is Mine, I will repay,' says the Lord." Romans 12:19 [NKJV].

Like a strong, cool breeze, I felt this passage from the

Holy Bible blow over my smoldering wrath and alleviate my pain. I now understand that murderers of human beings deserve death. When I am released this October, I will instead sue this man—just to hold him accountable for his actions. If I don't get the money, I'll just get on with my life.

Thank you for spreading God's Word, because God used you to deliver me from my misery and anger. Besides, I have a life-long goal of becoming a pediatric cardiologist to realize—something I could never achieve as a murderer.

If you feel small, weak, and foolish—move over! I'm right there with you! But the good news is that we're *exactly* the kind of people God chooses as His instruments to make a difference in the world. We are God's bright little pennies. God wants to do something great through small, weak, foolish creatures like you and me.

God is calling you and me to action on behalf of faith, family, and morality. But the action He calls us to does not involve strategies, tactics, intimidation, or force. God calls us to a firm but gentle, confident but humble activism. His model for a better future is not to defeat His enemies, but to win them over and make them His friends.

His model for action is a model of love.

Notes

Chapter 3: Living Healthy in an Unhealthy World

1. 1 Corinthians 3:16; 6:20 (NKJV).

Chapter 5: Staying Pure in a Polluted World

1. "Health News: Herpes on the Rise," *Parade Magazine*, February 8, 1998, p. 7.
2. Matthew 7:3–5 (NIV).
3. See 1 Corinthians 7:2–3.
4. See Genesis 1:27.
5. See Romans 1:24–32.
6. See Leviticus 18:20.
7. See Leviticus 18:6–18.
8. See Deuteronomy 23:17–18.
9. See Genesis 9:21–23.
10. See Romans 1:26–27.
11. See Matthew 5:27–28.
12. 1 Corinthians 6:13–20 (NKJV).
13. Patrick F. Fagan, "Why Religion Matters: The Impact of Religious Practice on Social Stability," *The Heritage Foundation Backgrounder No. 1064*, January 25, 1996, electronically retrieved from http://www.townhall.com/heritage/library/categories/family/bg1064.html.
14. Matthew 19:4–5 (NKJV).
15. Proverbs 5:18–19 (NKJV).
16. Philippians 4:8–9 (NKJV).

17. Ramona Cramer Tucker, "Enough is Enough: Donna Rice Hughes," *Today's Christian Woman,* September-October 1996, electronically retrieved from http://www.christianity.net/tcw/ 6W5/6W5042.html.

Chapter 6: Building Whole Families in a Broken World

1. Mark 10:8 (NKJV); cf. Genesis 2:24; Matthew 19:5–6; Ephesians 5:31.
2. Matthew 18:20 (NKJV).
3. Dr. James Osterhaus, *Questions Couples Ask Behind Closed Doors* (Wheaton, IL: Tyndale, 1996), pp. 2–3.
4. Nehemiah 4:14 (NKJV).

Chapter 7: Raising Safe, Strong Kids in a Dangerous World

1. Diane Loomans, "If I Had a Child to Raise Over Again," posted on Dr. Laura's website, electronically retrieved from http:// www.drlaura.com.

Chapter 8: Supermodel or Supermom—
What's a Career Mother to Do?

1. Melissa Healy, "A Less Taxing Approach to Daycare?" *The Los Angeles Times,* Monday, May 11, 1998, electronically retrieved fromhttp://www.latimes.com/HOME/NEWS/FRONT/t000044. 00.1.html.
2. Information electronically retrieved from http://www.womweb. com/wmdayc1.htm.
3. Quoted by Melissa Healy, "A Less Taxing Approach to Daycare?"

Chapter 9: A World of Equals

1. Matthew 7:12 (NKJV); see also Luke 6:31.

Chapter 10: Defending Life in a Dying World

1. Proverbs 24:11–12 (NKJV).
2. Hugo Gurdon and Norma McCorvey, "My Legal Fight . . . ,"

London Daily Telegraph, January 20, 1998, electronically retrieved at http://www.elibrary.com.

3. Ibid.
4. Ibid.
5. Michael Conlon, "Jane Roe 25 years later: 'I don't look back,'" Reuters, January 20, 1998, electronically retrieved at http://www.elibrary.com.
6. Ibid.
7. Gurdon and McCorvey, "My Legal Fight . . ."
8. Ellen Goodman, "The Ambivalence of Jane Roe," *St. Louis Post-Dispatch,* August 18, 1995, p. 7B, electronically retrieved at http://www.elibrary.com.
9. Rheta Grimsley Johnson, "Norma Wavers, But Roe Lives On," *The Atlanta Journal and Constitution,* August 14, 1995, p. B1, electronically retrieved at http://www.elibrary.com.
10. Psalm 51:14; 103:12 (NKJV).
11. Romans 5:8; 6:23 (NKJV).

Chapter 11: Defending Truth in a World of Lies

1. John 14:6 (NKJV).
2. John 8:31–32 (NKJV).
3. John 3:21 (NKJV).
4. Romans 1:20–22 (NKJV).
5. 2 Timothy 4:3–4 (NKJV).
6. 2 Timothy 3:7 (NKJV).
7. John Leo, "A No-Fault Holocaust," *U.S. News & World Report,* July 21, 1997, p. 14, electronically retrieved at http://www.elibrary.com.
8. Ginia Bellafante, "Bob Dole Is So Old That . . .—Finding Humor Beyond the Obvious, Comedy Central's Convention Coverage Is in Top Form," *Time,* August 26, 1996, p. 61.
9. See Ephesians 4:15.

Chapter 12: A Model for Action

1. 2 Chronicles 7:14 (NKJV).

2. Zechariah 4:6 (NKJV).
3. Luke 13:18–19 (NKJV).
4. 1 Corinthians 1:27 (NKJV).

About the Author

KIM ALEXIS has appeared on more than five hundred magazine covers. She is a spokesperson and spent three years as fashion editor on ABC's *Good Morning America*. She has hosted numerous cable TV shows, including *Healthy Kids* on the Family Channel and *Ticket to Adventure with Kim Alexis* on the Travel Channel as well as a parenting show on CBS. She is also a fitness/nutrition correspondent on *The 700 Club*. Her first book was a semiautobiographical novel, *With a Little Luck*. Kim and her husband, former hockey star Ron Duguay, live in southern California with their five children.

Printed in the United States
25097LVS00001B/474

9 780785 268574